The Beginnings of Christology

WILLI MARXSEN

The Beginnings of Christology

TOGETHER WITH

The Lord's Supper as a Christological Problem

Translated by
PAUL J. ACHTEMEIER and LORENZ NIETING

With an Introduction by
JOHN REUMANN

FORTRESS PRESS   PHILADELPHIA

This book is a reissue of two earlier volumes, *The Beginnings of Christology*, translated by Paul Achtemeier, copyright © 1969 by Fortress Press, and *The Lord's Supper as a Christological Problem,* translated by Lorenz Nieting, copyright © 1970 by Fortress Press. These volumes originally appeared in German as *Anfangsprobleme der Christologie* and *Das Abendmahl als christologisches Problem*, published by Gütersloher Verlagshaus, Gerd Mohn, in 1960 and 1963 respectively. They are translated here by arrangement with the publisher.

Library of Congress Cataloging in Publication Data

Marxsen, Willi, 1919-
  The beginnings of Christology, together with The Lord's Supper as a Christological problem.

    Translation of 2 works, Anfangsprobleme der Christologie and Das Abendmahl als christologisches Problem.
    Bibliography: p.
    1. Jesus Christ — History of doctrines — Early church, ca. 30-600 — Addresses, essays, lectures. 2. Lord's Supper — History — Early church, ca. 30-600 — Addresses, essays, lectures. I. Marxsen, Willi, 1919- Das Abendmahl als christologisches Problem. English. 1979.
    II. Title.
BT198.M39613 1979   232   79-7384
ISBN 0-8006-1372-4

7690B79   Printed in the United States of America   1-1372

Contents

Introduction

Christology—the ascription of honor, titles, and even deity to Jesus Christ for what he has done and who he is—is the proper frame of reference for treating the Lord's Supper, the meal begun by Jesus "on the night in which he was betrayed" for disciples in his fellowship, when he shared bread and wine with the blessing of God.

It is not always remembered that Albert Schweitzer wrote his famous sketch of the historical, messianic Jesus in 1901 within the context of a larger study on the problem of the Lord's Supper. To ask about Luther's Christology and his doctrine of the Lord's Supper is to raise a chicken-or-the-egg question, for it is debatable which influenced the other the more. Patristic understandings of the eucharist have often flowed from the christological metaphysics of the church fathers. Christology and the Lord's Supper interrelate.

Modern study of the New Testament, however, has frequently challenged whether Jesus himself shared any of the later notions about him as lord and Christ. Do such christological titles and the Lord's Supper of the early church go back to him during his historical lifetime?

It is an aim of the two essays which follow by Willi Marxsen, of Münster University, Germany, to show, in the wake of the New Quest for the historical Jesus, that there is a continuity between Jesus' ministry and the period after Easter. Even more so, he aims at pinpointing stages of development within the New Testament for Christology and the Lord's Supper.

The first and longer of the presentations, initially offered as lectures in 1959, reflects in more detail upon the methodology for such study. It probes three links between Jesus and the developments after Easter: that most difficult of all titles christologically, "Son of man"; the concept of faith; and, more briefly, the Lord's Supper.

The second essay, originally presented to pastors and ecumenical groups in Germany in 1962, expands upon the development of the Lord's Supper, especially in the thirties through the sixties of the first century, as we can perceive this from our New Testament sources. There are also some penetrating suggestions about consequences for today.

Overall, we meet with certain characteristic features of Professor Marxsen's work, as seen in other publications of his (see "For Further Reading" at the end of this book): the importance of the resurrection, the distinction between early Christian oral traditions and the editing treatment of them by an apostle or evangelist, the emphasis upon varieties of proclamation within the New Testament, and the way "the cause or purpose or content of Jesus goes on" from his earthly ministry through the later church.

In Christology, traditionally, on the view expounded in the Gospels themselves, Jesus is held to have claimed he was the Christ, the Son of man, lord, and Son of God during his earthly ministry. Hence the refinements worked out in succeeding generations, down through the Council of Chalcedon in A.D. 451, were felt to be but elaborations of what Jesus himself believed and taught. He was already the object of faith during his lifetime. He instituted the sacraments for the church he founded.

Critical study of the New Testament, however, beginning especially in the eighteenth century under rationalistic Deism, challenged this view increasingly. The human side of Jesus was emphasized more and more. It was asked whether Jesus actually said and did certain of the things attributed to him. In the nineteenth century the Gospel of John was marked off from the Synoptics and often set aside as a source about the historical Jesus. Sources within the Synoptics were posited. By the turn of the century some scholars, like William Wrede, were asking whether Jesus had thought of himself as anything more than a teacher — certainly not a messiah.

Form criticism — the subdiscipline of analyzing how stories about Jesus and sayings attributed to him developed in the oral period, before such material was written down in the early church — heightened the questions about accepting certain sayings as literal words of Jesus, or narratives as eyewitness verbatim reports. Instead it was argued that

such materials had been influenced by several decades of retelling in
the early church, and in some cases that the traditions had arisen
after Easter for community purposes. Thus the verses in Paul and the
Synoptics about the Last Supper were described as "etiological cult
legends," that is, accounts arising within the cultic community of Christians to explain an origin for the practice of taking bread and wine
during a meal and associating them with Jesus' body and blood, the
covenant, and forgiveness.

It is not surprising that some scholars therefore came to make a
sharp distinction between the historical Jesus and post-Easter Christology. Following Wrede's lead, they held that Jesus himself had been
an itinerant Jewish preacher who announced God's eschatological reign
and will. "The kingdom of God is at hand, repent!" Only after the
resurrection did the church in its Easter kerygma begin to proclaim him
Christ and lord. Rudolf Bultmann in particular articulated such a view.

The study of Christology in that way became accustomed to attribut-
ing few or none of the traditional messianic titles to the historical Jesus.
Only after the resurrection event did use of such honorifics arise. Only
with Easter did the man from Nazareth who had proclaimed God's
kingdom become the object of the church's proclamation. He who had
urged faith in God became now the center of faith.

Scholars have further sought to sketch stages of development for
Christology in the early church leading to the Gospels. First there was a
time in the thirties when faith in Jesus as the Messiah was confined to
Aramaic-speaking Jews in Palestine. Then the new faith spread to
Hellenized Jews in Palestine and in the Diaspora. Finally the new religion about Jesus emerged in the Gentile world. Specific titles for Jesus
and ways of speaking about him could with some confidence be associated with one of the stages or another. To speak of the "Son of man" or
the "covenant" reflects Semitic, not Greek, thinking. Terminology
about "the lord" at a cultic meal was said to stem from the Hellenistic
world. About a title such as "Son of God" debate often raged, for it
could be understood in Old Testament or in Greco-Roman categories.

To be sure, many, especially in the Anglo-Saxon countries, never
accepted such a radical reading of the beginning of Christology. They
continued to trace the titles fully back to Jesus' lifetime. Others allowed
the likelihood of post-Easter development but continued to put the

origins during the ministry of Jesus, seeds which grew later into the flourishing plant of Christology.

Just as it seemed as if the point of view which severs all or most Christology from the historical Jesus had won the day, at least in continental scholarship and above all in the Bultmann school on both sides of the Atlantic, a reaction set in, surprisingly in the ranks of Bultmann's own pupils. A "New Quest" for the historical Jesus was touched off by a paper read in 1953 by Professor Ernst Käsemann. For both historical and theological reasons, a new concern ensued to recover something of the human figure who stood behind the Christology of the Easter kerygma, in order to underscore again the continuity between Jesus' own words and deeds and the church's message about him. Must not the Nazarene proclaimer have been something akin to the Christ proclaimed and praised by the successive periods of early church development?

Needless to say, this so-called New Quest soon became a broad umbrella covering a variety of views, some of them of dubious historical — and theological — credentials. Against even some of the best and most heralded results of the current quest — for example, Günther Bornkamm's book *Jesus of Nazareth* — objections can be raised, as Marxsen indicates. Eventually the New Quest fragmented in a variety of directions.

Professor Marxsen's 1959 lectures fall generally within the New Quest. They are somewhat critical of the Bultmannian position, reopening old questions in new ways, with different answers. In general Marxsen seeks to describe what it is within the ministry of Jesus which can be said to have led to other developments after Easter. "Son of man," the concept of faith, and the meal are discussed for possible links. Since Marxsen often assumes some knowledge of scholarly debate on these topics, key items in the literature are listed under "For Further Reading."

Subsequent writings by Professor Marxsen argue for both a *Jesus-kerygma* and a post-Easter *Christ-kerygma*. There was, he insists, an "event" of Jesus of Nazareth, who proclaimed the kingdom and whose activities pointed to it. There is also a kerygma after Easter about the crucified Jesus as risen and exalted One. Marxsen has sought to distinguish his Jesus-kerygma as soteriologically grounded Christology and his Christ-kerygma as christologically grounded soteriology. (See especially his article on early Christian kerygmata in the *Zeitschrift für Theologie und Kirche* in 1976, cited at the er. 1 of this volume.)

Marxsen has, in his later writings, beginning with those on the resurrection, popularized the phrase in German *"die Sache Jesu"* to express this continuity between the earthly Jesus and the risen lord. "The 'cause of Jesus' goes on" in the usual rendering. *Sache* implies "purpose," "intent," even "Jesus *movement.*" Literally, "the 'Jesus thing' marches on." Catholic commentators (see "For Further Reading") in particular have been interested in this term of continuity between Jesus and the church. For Walter Kasper it is an example of "Christology from below," that is, a christological development which starts with the man Jesus and not from a figure with God above in heaven. Marxsen's treatment of the resurrection has been an object of some controversy. On the basis of his *Sache Jesu* theme, Watson has written that Marxsen no more minimizes Easter faith than T. W. Manson did.

In connection with the Lord's Supper, the words of Jesus in the Upper Room and the development of the meal in earliest Christianity have long been an interest of Professor Marxsen. His dissertation at Kiel in 1951 dealt with "the words of institution" (résumé in *Theologische Literaturzeitung* 77 [1952]: cols. 572-74). As early as 1952 he published an article in *Evangelische Theologie* (12 [1952-53]: 293-303) on the origins of the Lord's Supper. In the essay which concludes this volume, Marxsen elaborates in more popular terms on what he had said briefly about the Lord's Supper as one of his examples of christological links between Jesus and the church. A subsequent and even briefer treatment by Marxsen, originally for a radio audience in 1966, has also appeared in English in the volume from the German series "Kontexte," *Jesus in His Time.*

It is worth recalling that over the years there has been, in studying Christian origins, an immense amount of work on the beginnings of what we call holy communion or the eucharist. ("The Lord's Supper," I Corinthians 11:20, is a New Testament term. "Communion" occurs at I Corinthians 10:16, RSV note. "Eucharist," literally "thanksgiving" for God's benefits, becomes, it is agreed, a technical term for the meal and its elements only in the second century.) Schweitzer in 1901 felt he was contributing a new analysis of the words of institution in what was already a long history of interpretation. Since his day still other historical insights have emerged, notably from the isolation of pre-Pauline formulas dating from the decades before I Corinthians was written. Since Marxsen assumes much of this research, a few words on background may be in order here.

Paul and the three Synoptic Gospels record the institution by Jesus of the Lord's Supper, each somewhat differently. Paul writes of it at I Corinthians 11:23-25 in the context of rebuke for unruly disturbances which mar the meal-celebrations of the congregation at Corinth (the key verses are quoted on pp. 92-93 below). At I Corinthians 10:16 Paul also cites what is now regarded as another formula concerning "the cup of blessing which we bless" and "the bread which we break."

Mark recounts the institution of the sacrament on the night before Jesus' death (Passover, Nisan 15, in Mark's own chronology) at 14:22-24 (quoted below, p. 92). The key words are:

> This is my body. . . .
> This is my blood of the covenant, which is poured out for many.

Matthew reflects Mark's version, but with some variations in detail. Matthew has (26:26-28):

> This is my body. . . .
> This is my blood of the covenant, which is poured out for many for the forgiveness of sins.

Luke, while similar at points, presents the most puzzling text. He speaks of a cup which Jesus has the disciples divide among themselves (22:17-18) and then of bread over which Jesus says (22:19a):

> This is my body.

At that point the RSV and the NEB (but not the NAB or the TEV, among recent translations) place verses 19b and 20 in a footnote on the grounds that not all manuscripts contain the words. A majority of recent scholars, however, including most of the editors of the United Bible Societies' Greek New Testament text, are convinced that this "longer text" (including 19b-20) is what Luke wrote and that only an errant strain of the text tradition omitted it (so Joachim Jeremias,

Eduard Schweizer). The key words in Luke's long text then run (22: 19-20):

> This is my body which is given for you.
> This cup which is poured out for you is the new covenant in my blood.

All of these versions should be compared with the form Paul reports at I Corinthians 11:24-25:

> This is my body which is for you. . . .
> This cup is the new covenant in my blood.

The Gospel of John in its scene in the Upper Room (Nisan 14 in the Johannine chronology) has no institution of a meal-sacrament (chap. 13). But in John 6, in a discourse at Capernaum, Jesus is portrayed as speaking about "living bread" which, if a man eats, he will live forever, and Jesus identifies this bread as "my flesh" (6:51); he also speaks of drinking "my blood" (6:53-56). Bultmann has disputed whether verses 51b-58 are an original part of the book. Even if the verses are an insertion to bring this Gospel more in line with emerging church views, John speaks about bread of life, and blood which brings life—even if there are no words of institution in the Upper Room.

Many attempts have been made to bring all these passages (and those in documents outside the New Testament) together in a comprehensive way. Jeremias has studied them in order to recover the earliest possible form in Aramaic which Jesus could have spoken. The survey by Schweizer reports on various theories advanced about the biblical reports on the institution of the Lord's Supper, as does a more recent encyclopedia article by Gerhard Delling. Form criticism is responsible for the contention that each version reflects the wording in use by some segment of the early church, with the implication that perhaps no one account goes back verbatim to Jesus. Thus we would have cult legends used by four different New Testament writers, each in his own situation. Even a cursory glance at the words of institution shows that the versions in Mark and Matthew can be grouped together, that Paul differs, and that the Lucan form has affinities to Paul. But the order and relationships among these Lord's Supper formulas have never been established to everyone's satisfaction. It is one of Marxsen's endeavors to try to do so.

One classic effort to unravel the relation of various Lord's Supper references in the New Testament and other early Christian records and set them in some sequence showing the development of this sacrament is the monograph by Hans Lietzmann, *Mass and Lord's Supper* (1926). Lietzmann began with the liturgical materials of later centuries and tried to work backwards to the New Testament period. Here he concluded for two types of meal-celebrations in earliest Christianity.

The first Lietzmann called the Jerusalem type because it is exemplified by the practice of the Jerusalem church in the Book of Acts. It was said to stem from actual meals which Jesus practiced with his disciples during his lifetime—a *ḥaburah,* he and his intimate followers partaking of a fellowship meal together. After Easter this type of meal continued in the Jerusalem community in what the Acts of the Apostles calls the breaking of bread (2:42, 46), with emphasis on apocalyptic gladness and the joy of fellowship with the risen lord. Lietzmann found later examples in the Didache (an early Jewish-Christian writing) and the liturgy of Serapion in Egypt. The meal is central, a Lord's *Supper,* akin to the agape or "love feast"; no words of institution and no reference to the death, cross, or blood of Jesus.

Lietzmann's second type does contain words of institution, stressing Jesus' death as well as his resurrection and coming again. There is also prominence given to a new covenant established by his atoning death. These ideas appear in Paul's references in I Corinthians 10 and 11, in the Synoptic accounts, and in the later liturgy of Hippolytus and all subsequent liturgies derived from it, what subsequently comes to be called the mass.

"Mass" and "Lord's *Supper*" thus both derive from New Testament times. Lietzmann allowed for influence on each type out of the Hellenistic world. The Jerusalem meal could reflect the Hellenistic notion that a sacrifice indwelt by the name or power of a god conferred certain benefits. The Pauline type took on characteristics of memorial meals practiced in certain Greco-Roman groups ("This do in remembrance of me"). One controversial feature of Lietzmann's analysis—on which few subsequent scholars have followed him—is that Paul himself added this phrase in I Corinthians 11:24–25, "Do this in remembrance of me," and focused attention on the lord's death and coming again (vs. 26) on the strength of a direct revelation from the risen Christ (cf. 11:23, "I received *from the Lord,*" that is, direct, not via the oral tradition). Most commentators feel Paul is employing at 11:23-25 a tradition transmitted to him from other Christians and that Paul saw the Lord Jesus not only at the beginning of the process of traditioning but also in it, giving life and power to it, as lord.

To be sure, many scholars dispute Lietzmann's reconstruction at a variety of points, though admitting there has been a course of development, a "Lord's Supper 'trajectory.'" Other investigators have sought to build upon his work. In the 1930s Ernst Lohmeyer connected Lietzmann's Jerusalem type with Galilean Christianity as he reconstructed it, and Lietzmann's second type with Jerusalem. Oscar Cullmann has posited as roots for the sacrament which developed in the church not only the Upper Room but also meals Jesus celebrated with his *ḥaburah* during his ministry, and postresurrection meals of the risen lord with his disciples (Luke 24:36 ff.; Acts 1:4). The lengthy essay by Robert Douglas Richardson attached to the English translation of Lietzmann — a "Further Inquiry into Eucharistic Origins," begun by Richardson in the 1940s and published and extended in stages till the 1970s — differs on any "radical duality of rite from the beginning" but does seek to trace two lines of interpretation in the New Testament. The one, according to Richardson, is to be seen in Mark 14 and I Corinthians 11, stressing words of institution, wine, and the death of Jesus; the other emphasizes bread and Jesus' risen presence but has no words of institution. The former, Richardson claims, gave distinctive character to liturgies of Western Christianity, the latter to liturgies of the East.

It is into a thicket of such theories that Marxsen enters in treating the origins of the Lord's Supper within the framework of developing Christology. We may illustrate how views contrast by one example. I Corinthians 11:23-26, Richardson argues, is not part of the Letter Paul wrote but an interpolation from the latter half of the second century, of Roman origin. (There is no manuscript evidence for such a view, and Richardson overlooks the fact that what Paul writes in vss. 27-32 depends on ideas and phrases in vss. 23-26.) Much more likely is the view of recent New Testament scholarship that 11:23-25 is a pre-Pauline quotation from common Christian tradition, like I Corinthians 15:3-5.

Clues for a pre-Pauline formula in 11:23-25 include the way it is introduced, the vocabulary employed, and the fact that words and ideas in the formula differ from the immediate context and from Paul's own usage. The passage begins: "I *received* what I *delivered* to you," employing the technical terms for passing on a tradition orally in rabbinic and Greek Christian use (cf. Jeremias). Words like "give thanks," "remembrance," and "after supper" are either unique to this passage or not normally employed thus by Paul. In verse 24 "body of Christ" refers to Jesus' earthly body on the cross, whereas normally for Paul "body of Christ" means the Christian community (12:12 ff., especially vs. 27). This is the sort of evidence, painstakingly worked through by other scholars, which Marxsen assumes, so that 11:23-25 can be termed an earlier formula Paul quotes to begin his discussion, with comment beginning in verse 26.

The same sort of analysis may be assumed for I Corinthians 10:16, where the formula which Paul cites presumably ran:

> The cup of blessing which we bless is a participation in the blood of Christ (is it not?).
> The bread which we break is a participation in the body of Christ (is it not?).

Paul has reversed the usual sequence of bread/cup here because he wishes to attach a comment on the bread-word in verse 17.

Professor Marxsen has himself been a contributor to such literary analysis of the New Testament with his pioneer redaction-critical work on the Gospel of Mark. His views on every New Testament writing can be checked in his *Introduction to the New Testament*, which has enjoyed widespread use in both German and English. Yet he has also exhibited in his writings a concern for problems of today in the church, as his closing remarks in the essay on the Lord's Supper show (addressed to the German scene, but of interest in other parts of the world). One reviewer of Marxsen's essays on the exegete as theologian commended both his scientific passion and his theological responsibility, not to mention his pastoral concern and even caution.

The translation of the first essay is the work of Dr. Paul J. Achtemeier, now teaching at Union Theological Seminary, Richmond, Virginia, and the second of Dr. Lorenz Nieting, Professor of New Testament at the Lutheran Theological Seminary, Gettysburg, Pennsylvania. Parallel references to a passage in one Synoptic Gospel, where not cited by chapter and verse, are indicated by the abbreviation "par." Scriptural quotations are usually from the RSV. Conventional English renderings for technical terms about the Lord's Supper such as occur in translations of Jeremias and Schweitzer—like "words of interpretation" for *Deutewort* and "word over the bread" for *Brotwort*—have been followed. Minor corrections have been made in the essays for this reprinting, and the bibliographies, notes, and introduction have been revised.

JOHN REUMANN

Lutheran Theological Seminary
Philadelphia
January 1979

PART ONE

The Beginnings
of
Christology

On Methodology

Up to the present time, New Testament research has been unable to come to any generally acknowledged consensus concerning the point at which Christology begins, whether with Jesus himself, or only after Easter in the primitive Christian community. This alternative is the result of divergent historical judgments. The situation is not such, however, that one needs simply to intensify the research in order finally to arrive at agreement. The problem lies at a deeper level, and thus proves to be more complicated. In view of the character of the material to be investigated, we must seek to clarify what historical research is capable of accomplishing in this instance, and where the limits are to be found beyond which such questioning may not go. The question of content shows itself to be closely connected with the question of method. It is with this latter question that we must first occupy ourselves. We shall have to limit ourselves, however, to a development of the most important points.

In the foreword to his *Christology of the New Testament,* Oscar Cullmann says his book is "an exegetical work,"[1] and he asks of his critics that they "not dispose of [his] interpretations with apodictic assertions and verdicts without exegetical grounds."[2] That seems so obvious a request one would think it hardly worth mentioning. And yet it is easy to conceal a problem here. Exegesis, of course, enables us to discern the later Christology, that of the primitive Christian community. I should like to maintain, however, that it is absolutely impossible to answer the question concerning the beginning of Christology by means of exegesis of the New Testament.

---

1. O. Cullmann, *The Christology of the New Testament,* trans. Shirley C. Guthrie and Charles A. M. Hall (Philadelphia: Westminster, 1959, ²1963), p. xiii.
    2. *Ibid.*

In all likelihood, this claim will appear surprising. For that reason, I shall justify it very briefly. By "exegesis" I understand the task of repeating[3] in my own language what the author wanted to say to his readers. Exegesis, therefore, has to do with *the text which lies before us* in its present form and in its present context. For that reason I emphasize that the task of exegesis is to reproduce the *author's* statements. With respect to the Synoptic Gospels, that means we are concerned with the statements of the final editors.

Even though individual results of New Testament research into the history of the editorial process (*Redaktionsgeschichte*) may be disputed, we have nevertheless learned the basic fact that "Mark," "Matthew," and "Luke" have ordered, connected, commented upon, and in part also shaped, their sources in light of particular theological conceptions. These conceptions were rooted in the situation of the given author and his readers. The works are therefore written with a *specific* audience in view. Exegesis dare not leave this out of account.

The New Testament texts are not addressed to me. Whether or not they will address me *after* the work of exegesis is done is another matter. In any case, the author's statements, which exegesis lifts into prominence and repeats after him, do not have to do with me. Exegesis involves me only insofar as *I* am the one who does the exegesis—it is *my* language and *my* concepts in which the old statements are rephrased.

It may well be that this definition of exegesis will be regarded as too narrow. It is my opinion, however, that nowadays an important step is all too easily overlooked if one does not differentiate with methodological clarity between understanding a text, and being addressed by it in a way that lays claim upon me. It seems to me that we have here one of the basic reasons for the oft-lamented tension between the exegete and the systematic theologian. Exegesis is not a specifically theological task, and the exegete does not necessarily have to be a theologian. If he is, of course he knows that the results of biblical exegesis have to become theologically relevant. But that is a next step and therefore should not have any effect on the exegete in his work. It is precisely this point that our definition is intended to express.

I have said that the question concerning the beginning of Christology cannot be answered by means of exegesis. I think the reason for this

---

3. [The German word *nachsprechen*, "speaking or saying after" (i.e., repeating what someone has said), is rendered by "repeat" or "reproduce."—EDITOR.]

assertion is now evident. All the authors of New Testament writings proceed on the basis of some sort of christological conception. Accordingly, exegesis will continually reproduce this christological conception, but exegesis cannot take me back any further than to the composition of the oldest New Testament writing. Therefore, *on the basis of exegesis,* I can say only that the beginning of Christology has to lie before the time when I Thessalonians was written.

Is there, nevertheless, perhaps a possibility of penetrating back into an earlier period of time? That would be the case, if the writings themselves contained statements concerning this earlier time. In this respect the Letters of Paul have very little to contribute (at most, in a very indirect way); the Gospels on the other hand do (although they were written later!). The Gospels present Jesus christologically, or have Jesus himself make christological statements. This is an unambiguous finding of exegetical research. But it does not necessarily take us any further back, despite the Gospels' references to an earlier period, because, if we are to proceed with proper methodological caution, we must say that we are here dealing in the first instance with nothing more than statements of the Gospel writers. But does that mean we are dealing with information which is historically reliable?

When such doubts are raised, one should not immediately speak of skepticism. This exegetical finding simply brings home to us the critical question. To be sure, Matthew and Luke repeat Mark's christological statements, but many times these statements are no longer understood (e.g., the motif of the Messianic Secret), many times they are given another form and, in addition, are often supplemented by other statements. We have before us, therefore, an unfolding development, and that leads necessarily to the question whether Mark may not also reflect *one* stage of christological development. Exegesis will then bring out *this* stage. Our question, on the other hand, concerns the beginning of Christology.

We will be able to move further here only if we draw on material for comparison from an earlier period. This material, however, is not available to us in a separate form *alongside* the Gospels—it must be reconstructed out of the Gospels themselves. But here we are confronted by a difficulty. The Gospel writers have, to be sure, generally employed very simple literary methods in their editorial work. Nevertheless, it must be clearly understood, complete certainty in the isolating of sources cannot be attained. For that reason conclusions fluctuate, in some instances quite substantially.

After the sources have been isolated, another exegesis is possible. Attention must be paid to the fact that this second exegesis differs considerably from that of the New Testament documents as they stand. I have already indicated a basic difference: we must first reconstruct the texts for this exegesis. They are available to us only in a later version, reworked by an editor. What these sources seek to say does not, however, necessarily coincide with what the Gospel writers intend to say when they make use of these sources. Research into the history of the editorial process the Gospels have undergone has amply documented this. The point to be seen is that the decision about the beginning of Christology has to do, not with the exegesis of the New Testament texts as they now stand, but with material prior to the present form of the New Testament.

There are, among the sources of the Synoptic Gospels, certain passages which either are not christologically determined or in which (at least at first glance) no reference to Christology is discernible. One could point here, for example, to the Sermon on the Mount, to the speeches against the Pharisees, to some of the parables, indeed to a large portion of the material containing sayings of Jesus. When we do an exegesis of these passages, we must ask whose statements we want to reproduce in this instance. Unfortunately, this question is all too often not raised. It is, however, of considerable significance. If we do our exegesis within the context of the New Testament as it lies before us, then we find that these passages, in which there is no discernible reference to christological affirmation, are nevertheless not without this reference. He who speaks these words, namely, Jesus, is always seen by the Gospel writers in a christological context. It is just this point that exegesis must take into account. Whoever, for example, would limit himself in the exegesis of the Sermon on the Mount to these three chapters, but would exclude the Matthean Christology which has found a particularly clear expression in the Old Testament "formula quotations" (of which there are no examples in the Sermon on the Mount), that person has by no means exegeted chapters 5–7 as composed by *Matthew*. Rather, he has isolated a portion of a work, which the editor of that work intended to be understood in its context. Or he has gone back behind the Gospel. Of course, in that case he is no longer dealing with the Sermon on the

Mount but with individual passages, because the composition of that Sermon is the work of the evangelist.

There are, therefore, in individual passages, a large number of older portions of tradition which do not show any relationship to Christology. But one must, of course, immediately add that other sources, which can similarly be reconstructed on the basis of literary-critical work, do make christological statements. But we now face the real problem. Exegesis of the Synoptic Gospels confronts us with the assertion that Christology begins with Jesus. Exegesis of the sources establishes that before the existence of the New Testament there were traditions which betray no relationship to Christology, as well as other traditions which contain christological statements. It is necessary, therefore, to arrange these various sources in chronological order. But to do so is to add a second difficulty to the first (the isolating of the sources): it is by no means simple to find truly reliable criteria for dating the early traditions.

In the light of our findings (which we have sketched out only very roughly) one *could* argue that apparently there is a tendency toward christologizing. One would then have to conclude that the non-christological sources are the older; the process of christologizing begins only at a later date. That would mean that at some point a break in continuity occurred. But here again objections can be raised. Is it not more likely that there was a continuous development? One can, moreover, ask why all traditions should *have* to contain Christology. Alongside of old, christological sources there would then also have been sources without a specifically christological orientation.

That is assumed by almost all Anglo-Saxon theologians, and also by many German scholars. (The form critics—in Germany—constitute almost the only exception.) If a continuous development is assumed, then Christology begins with Jesus. He understood himself as the *'Ebed Yahweh*[4] or as the Son of man, or he used both titles with reference to himself. The primitive Christian community took up this usage, preserved it, but then later developed it too.

It must be conceded that this solution commends itself quite strongly because it reckons with a continuous development, one which can then

4. [Hebrew, "Servant of Yahweh," the figure appearing in certain passages in Isaiah, 42:1-4, 49:1-6, 50:4-11, 52:13—53:12. —EDITOR.]

be retraced. An uncritical observer will always regard this solution as the most natural one. It must also be conceded that very weighty arguments are required if one desires to replace this solution with another which, in the place of continuity, would posit discontinuity — a solution which sees a break between Jesus and the primitive Christian community, which allows Christology to begin only after Easter, within the primitive Christian community, and which sketches the picture of the historical Jesus in a non-christological way.

Yet that is just what has been done through form criticism. I need not retrace the history of form criticism in its particulars. We may simply remind ourselves that form criticism was the result of historical research into the New Testament texts. The intention was to reach back to the historical Jesus. When, about the turn of the century, the two-document hypothesis[5] was generally accepted, it was believed that the goal was about to be reached. Then, however, it was shown (by K. L. Schmidt) that the framework of the story of Jesus had to be discounted, even the Marcan framework. It proved to be impossible to write a life of Jesus. One could ask historical questions only of the individual units of material. This questioning, however, did not enable one to arrive at the historical Jesus. Instead, one found the kerygma, the *Sitz im Leben,* the primitive Christian community. It was recognized that the community was not motivated by historical interests in its portrayal of Jesus; rather, the individual units of tradition served the task of preaching. Thus there was a limit to how far back one could go historically. One could no longer get back behind Easter by historical means. At the beginning stood the Easter faith of the community.

We must here, however, take into account one element which, to the detriment of the subject matter, has frequently been overlooked. The conclusions of form criticism must not be confused with a historical judgment concerning the *content* of the units of tradition. That the material was formed in the community, that it was shaped in the light of a *Sitz im Leben,* that it was formulated for the purpose of preaching (understood in its widest sense as proclamation in a variety of forms), all of that does *not* mean that, as a result, the content of this preaching,

---

5. [The theory that Mark (or an earlier form of Mark) and Q (a collection of Jesus' sayings) were the two written sources for the Synoptic Gospels. — EDITOR.]

insofar as it concerns Jesus, *must* be unhistorical. Neither does it mean, of course, that this content is a faithful historical reproduction of what happened.

We must here take into account the fact that the historical question, as we pose it, and as we must pose it if we want to reach a historical result, was at that time still unknown. We must further take into account that our sources cannot even be classified within the framework of ancient historical writing. Therefore, if we today arrive at a historical judgment on the basis of these texts, then we have approached them with a form of questioning which is foreign to the sources themselves, which the authors and bearers of these traditions were not able to take into account in their presentations, to say nothing of wanting to do so.

The *Sitz im Leben* is the final point which can be reached directly by means of historical investigation. If I want to go beyond that, then I must search for historical proof. If I want to declare something to be historical, I must prove it. If I want to declare something to be unhistorical, I must prove that too. And I must carry out both proofs in such a way that they can be checked by any given historian.

That appears to me to be the conclusion—a clearly exciting conclusion—to be drawn from form criticism. We stand here before a barrier, but not because we delight in skepticism. How would one justify such a stance? We stand before the barrier because we are posing questions in a way which is foreign to the text itself.

That does not mean that our question is on principle excluded. But it may be illuminating to note that in face of this difficulty, the answers diverge from one another, at times substantially. Here I can only pursue the discussion to the extent that is necessary for attaining a point of departure. We must begin with Rudolf Bultmann.

Does the beginning of Christology lie with Jesus? Did Jesus apply any messianic title to himself? Bultmann says rightly: "Only the historian can answer this question—as far as it can be answered at all."[6]

Despite this restriction, Bultmann attempts to give an answer. On a critical basis he works out the preaching of Jesus, with the result that in this preaching there is no portion which contains an explicit Christology. Only in the Christian community was Jesus' preaching "taken up

6. R. Bultmann, *Theology of the New Testament*, trans. Kendrick Grobel, Vol. 1 (New York: Scribner's, 1951), p. 26.

again, in the form (and thus it became 'Christian' preaching) that he, the proclaimer, was included in the proclamation as the one who is proclaimed."[7] True Christology begins therefore only in the Christian community.

For this reason, Jesus' preaching does not belong within the framework of New Testament theology. Bultmann discusses it within the framework of the Jewish religion. Nevertheless, Jesus' preaching is the presupposition of New Testament theology. That is true in a twofold way. On the one hand, the preaching of Jesus contains an implicit Christology, which is made explicit by the early church. On the other hand, Bultmann emphasizes that theology cannot give up Jesus altogether, insofar as it is concerned with the "that"[8] of his humanity. Bultmann, therefore, wants by all means to prevent the mythicizing of the kerygma, and strongly emphasizes that the revelation of God occurred in a man, and therefore within history. But anything more than this "that" is of no significance. Jesus' self-understanding or his self-consciousness is theologically of no value whatsoever. What can be said about the historical Jesus belongs in the realm of the *Christos kata sarka*.[9] That Christ, however, "does not concern us," says Bultmann. "What went on within Jesus' own heart I do not know and I do not want to know."[10] Thus, the significance of Jesus for theology is reduced to a minimum, and the question has been asked whether there does not lurk here a "kerygma-theological Docetism."[11] Before we follow that line of thought, however, let us turn first to the historical problem.

7. R. Bultmann, *Das Urchristentum im Rahmen der antiken Religionen* (2d ed.; Zurich: Artemis Verlag, 1954), p. 100; trans. R. H. Fuller, *Primitive Christianity in Its Contemporary Setting* (New York: Meridian Books, 1956), p. 93: Jesus' "preaching was thus taken up in a new form, thus becoming specifically 'Christian' preaching. Jesus proclaimed the message. The Church proclaims *him*."

8. [German, *das Dass*, the fact "that" Jesus lived as a historical person, as distinguished from the "what" or the "how" of his life story. Cf. R. Bultmann, "The Primitive Christian Kerygma and the Historical Jesus," in *The Historical Jesus and the Kerygmatic Christ*, trans. and ed. Carl E. Braaten and Roy A. Harrisville (Nashville: Abingdon, 1964), pp. 20 ff. — EDITOR.]

9. ["Christ after the flesh," II Cor. 5:16, a phrase often used in the Bultmann School in a disparaging sense for the "biographical Jesus." — EDITOR.]

10. R. Bultmann, "Zur Frage der Christologie," in *Glauben und Verstehen*, Vol. 1 (2d ed.; Tübingen: Mohr, 1954), p. 101.

11. Cf. N. A. Dahl, "The Problem of the Historical Jesus," in *Kerygma and History*, trans. and ed. Carl E. Braaten and Roy A. Harrisville (Nashville: Abingdon, 1962), p. 161.

It is clear that as far as Bultmann is concerned one cannot speak of an absolute discontinuity between Jesus and the church. To be sure, there is a
break between Jesus and the church (the one who proclaimed becomes
the one who is proclaimed). But by emphasizing the "that" of the humanity of Jesus, and by means of the formula "implicit-explicit Christology,"
this abyss is bridged, however slender that bridge may be. One can postulate this abyss, however, only if one is able to describe what lies behind
it. Can that be done, despite the insights resulting from form criticism?

Bultmann has described, in three different places, the preaching of
Jesus. First (and in this instance without any attempt to give a coherent
picture) in the historical judgments contained in his book *The History
of the Synoptic Tradition;* later, in his book *Jesus and the Word;* and,
finally, in his *Primitive Christianity in Its Contemporary Setting* and (at
about the same time) in his *Theology of the New Testament.*[12] Can we
discern the criteria which underlie his historical judgments?

In his book about Jesus, Bultmann is still very careful. In the foreword to the book, he discusses the problem at some length. He asks
about the oldest stratum of early Christian preaching and sees quite
clearly that one cannot differentiate with any exactitude between the
preaching done by the church and the preaching of Jesus. His intention
is simply to present the oldest stratum of tradition, and referring to the
title of his book, he says, "Whoever prefers to put the name of 'Jesus'
always in quotation marks and let it stand as an abbreviation for the
historical phenomenon with which we are concerned, is free to do so."[13]
This qualification means, therefore, that the results of form criticism
are here taken seriously.

Unfortunately, however, Bultmann did not retain these quotation
marks. That becomes quite plain when he describes the preaching of
Jesus within the framework of the Jewish religion in his book on primitive Christianity. It would be highly interesting to indicate in detail
what this proclamation looks like and how it is arrived at. In this instance, I can only indicate the result.

---

12. *The History of the Synoptic Tradition* (German, 1921), trans. John Marsh (New
York: Harper & Row, 1963); *Jesus and the Word* (German, 1926), trans. L. Smith and
E. Huntress (New York: Scribner, 1934); *Primitive Christianity* (German, 1949; see
above, n. 7); *Theology* (German, 1948–51; see above, n. 6).

13. *Jesus and the Word* (cited above, n. 12), p. 14. The title of the original German
volume was simply *Jesus.*

Jesus' proclamation, as presented by Bultmann, is characterized by a noteworthy unity. Does that, however, indicate historical authenticity? Other descriptions of Jesus' preaching, which choose different elements from the sources, are also able to give the impression of unity. With this observation, however, we have already indicated the decisive point. The proclamation of Jesus is arrived at by eliminating all those passages which are tendentious, that is to say, by eliminating all those passages which represent, in Bultmann's opinion, a conception held by the primitive Christian community, but not the conception held by Jesus himself.

But what is the source from which Bultmann gains this criterion? Form criticism cannot have given it to him, since form criticism leads back only to the primitive community. To be sure, one can establish certain interests which existed in the primitive community, and therefore a tendency which had been there from a very early time. But what is the source of this tendency? That appears to me to be the decisive question.

If I postulate (and in face of the form-critical result it *is* a postulate) that the tendency arose for the first time within the primitive Christian community, then I set aside all passages which contain this tendency and allow to stand only those which either do not contain this tendency or in which I do not recognize it. When my point of departure is, therefore, this sort of discontinuity, then, quite naturally, I arrive in the end at a discontinuity. My result was already my presupposition. The reverse is also true.

For that reason, it is my opinion that one cannot in this way cross over the abyss of discontinuity. By that I do not intend to say that all of Bultmann's historical judgments are false, but I do believe that, because of the character of our sources, the judgments are much too uncertain to allow one to write a fullblown description, based on those sources, of the preaching of Jesus, localizing this preaching in Judaism, and, on that basis, postulating a break which then leads to a discontinuity in Christology. On the other hand, however, I have never been able really to understand why Bultmann is so often accused of historical skepticism. The extent of the material concerning Jesus which is in his judgment authentic is quite large, much larger than it actually could be if form criticism were applied consistently. I do not mean to say, contrariwise, that this material is in large part nonhistorical. It is my opinion, how-

ever, that Bultmann's conclusions place us once more before the necessity of discussing the question of method.

That is recognized at the present time in many quarters. Thus, the
quest of the historical Jesus has been set in motion anew since the article
by Ernst Käsemann.[14] This new interest in the historical Jesus is dependent, not least, upon a reflection of a systematic character. Interpreters
are no longer so ready as Bultmann to limit the significance of Jesus for
theology to the simple "that" of his humanity. At the very least, such a
view does not take sufficient account of the interest of the Gospel writers
and their sources. Despite the orientation of each to his particular environment (an orientation conditioned by proclamation), none of them
suppresses the fact that what is proclaimed bears a relationship to the
past. Käsemann puts it thus: "Because primitive Christianity experienced the earthly history of Jesus . . . as *kairos,* it wrote Gospels and
did not after Easter simply let the life story of Jesus go by the board."[15]

If, then, one desires, for theological reasons, to "expand" the Bultmannian "that," such expansion can be accomplished only by following the path of historical investigation. If one sees in Bultmann the
danger of a "kerygma-theological Docetism" (one cannot reasonably
speak of more than a danger), that danger can be averted only if one is
not moved by anxiety in face of possible consequences to cast overboard
all methodological care in dealing with the historical question. It appears to me that particular care is necessary here, precisely because we
may be on the way to overcoming the separation of the theological and
the historical question concerning Jesus—as it appears in Bultmann—
by allowing the historical question to enter into the theological question. Is such care, however, actually practiced at the present time?

Paul Althaus, for example, maintains that certain basic elements of
the New Testament picture of Jesus cannot have been invented.[16]
Günther Bornkamm says that the Gospels give us no justification for
resignation (in face of the historical question) and skepticism (with
respect to historical judgment). Quite the contrary, they "bring before
our eyes . . . the historical person of Jesus with the utmost vividness." He

14. "The Problem of the Historical Jesus," in Käsemann's *Essays on New Testament
Themes,* trans. W. J. Montague ("Studies in Biblical Theology," 41 [Naperville, Ill.:
Allenson, 1964]), pp. 15–47.

15. *Ibid.,* p. 31.

16. *Fact and Faith in the Kerygma of Today,* trans. David Cairns (Philadelphia:
Muhlenberg, 1959), pp. 73 f.

then continues: "Quite clearly what the Gospels report concerning the
message, the deeds, and the history of Jesus is still distinguished by an
authenticity, a freshness, and a distinctiveness not in any way effaced by
the Church's Easter faith. These features point us directly to the earthly
figure of Jesus."[17] But are these the kind of criteria which can really
withstand a critical historical investigation? Bornkamm himself con-
cedes that "mathematical certainty in the exposition of a bare history of
Jesus, unembellished by faith, is unobtainable, in spite of the fact that
the critical discernment of older and more recent layers of tradition belongs to the work of research."[18] Stauffer's "iron rule," *in dubio pro
tradito*,[19] could be applied with profit only if our sources had *primarily*
historical interests. That, however, must be seriously questioned. For
that reason I also find it difficult to speak, with Bornkamm, about the
"double character" of the Gospels as "proclamation and report."[20] Here
the actual problem is hidden by the word "and." One has the impression
that one could ask at one time for the proclamation, at another time for
the report. In my opinion, however, one cannot simply place the motif
of proclamation alongside the motif of reporting. The primitive Christian community intended to proclaim, as Bornkamm correctly says,
who Jesus *is*, not who he *was*.[21] The tradition therefore takes the *form* of
proclamation; it is primarily interested in the present. In proclamation,
to be sure, the tradition holds fast to the *ephapax*,[22] but it presents the
contemporary meaning of Jesus at the very time that it portrays him as
a personage of the past. But since the tradition does not pose the modern
historical question, it can use material, in realizing that purpose, which
according to *our* judgment is historical or nonhistorical. With that observation, however, the whole question is once more thrown open.

Hans Conzelmann's methodological principle also fails, at least in my
opinion, to lead us to the kind of certainty which is necessary for a his-

17. G. Bornkamm, *Jesus of Nazareth,* trans. I. and F. McLuskey with J. M. Robinson
(New York: Harper, 1960), p. 24
18. *Ibid.,* p. 14.
19. E. Stauffer, "Der Stand der neutestamentlichen Forschung," in *Theologie und
Liturgie: Eine Gesamtschau der gegenwärtigen Forschung in Einzeldarstellungen* (Kassel:
Stauda-Verlag, 1952), pp. 35–106.
20. G. Bornkamm, "Evangelien, formgeschichtlich," in *Die Religion in Geschichte und
Gegenwart* (3d ed.; Tübingen: Mohr, 1957–1965), Vol. 2, col. 750.
21. G. Bornkamm, *Jesus of Nazareth* (cited above, n. 17), p. 17.
22. [Greek, "once for all" (Rom. 6:10; Heb. 7:27, 9:12, 10:10), a phrase expressing the
unique past action of God in Christ, the "once-for-all" nature of the "Christ event."
—EDITOR.]

torical judgment. He maintains that we can regard as genuinely from Jesus only what cannot be fitted into Jewish thought or into the views held by the later Christian community.[23] But this category would also include everything which (possibly) arose or was formulated in the earliest period of the primitive Christian community, perhaps on the basis of the Easter experience and in conjunction with the expectation of an immediate Parousia. This expectation stood, on the one hand, in contrast to Jewish concepts, but on the other hand could also not have been said, or have been said in that way, in the later Christian community. Thus we do not have by any means a sure, positive criterion with this methodological principle. Its value as a negative criterion is also limited. Can one really say that a given word was not spoken by Jesus simply because it fits into Jewish thinking? Of course, if a saying contains concepts which arise only later in the Christian community, it can hardly be attributed to Jesus.

We may now seem to have run into a blind alley. We are not permitted, nor should we want, to give up posing historical *questions.* Must we nevertheless renounce historical *judgment* because of insufficient certainty? I do not believe such to be the case, even though the limits set up for form criticism will have to be observed more carefully. However, before I go into that, I should like to include some other points which concern our special problem, namely, the beginning of Christology. It is not always easy to recognize the dislocation of the crucial point in the way the question is raised.

I refer to some things that I have already mentioned. We have seen that, according to Bultmann, a discontinuity exists between Jesus and the primitive Christian community to the extent that the one who proclaimed became the one proclaimed. The implicit Christology which is found in Jesus' proclamation becomes in that manner explicit. Ernst Käsemann[24] and Günther Bornkamm[25] agree with Bultmann that Jesus did not refer any of the traditional titles to himself. To that extent it is

23. Hans Conzelmann, "Jesus Christus," in *Die Religion in Geschichte und Gegenwart* (cited above, n. 20), Vol 3 (1959), col. 623; Eng. trans. *Jesus: The classic article from RGG³ expanded and updated,* trans. J. Raymond Lord, ed. and with an intro. by John Reumann (Philadelphia: Fortress, 1973), p. 16; similarly now Gerhard Ebeling, *The Nature of Faith,* trans. Ronald G. Smith (Philadelphia: Muhlenberg, 1961), p. 52.

24. E. Käsemann (cited above, n. 14), pp. 43 f.

25. G. Bornkamm, *Jesus of Nazareth* (cited above, n. 17), p. 172.

necessary to speak of a transition from implicit to explicit Christology with respect to these scholars as well. Nevertheless, the discontinuity has now been modified.

Bultmann sees in the process of making the Christology explicit the *answer of the primitive community* to Jesus' call for decision. Here the decisive importance does not lie in the content of Jesus' proclamation; rather it is a matter of the "decision for his person as the bearer of the Word." It is precisely this decision which the primitive community made after Easter. Christology is thus the unfolding of "the implications of the positive answer to his demand for the decision."[26] This is significant. Bultmann presumes the call of Jesus to be historical,[27] but at the same time it remains — as historical call — without theological meaning, because it depends neither on its content nor on a self-consciousness of Jesus that could perhaps be lifted out of it. All this belongs, of course, in the realm of the *Christos kata sarka,* and does not concern us.[28] The historian, to be sure, can concern himself with that, as Bultmann (as a historian) in fact does, but "faith, being personal decision, cannot be dependent upon a historian's labor."[29]

But can the historical question really be excluded in such a manner from any relevance for theology? Above all (and more exactly formulated): is it permissible to exclude from relevance for theology the historical question *if* (in whatever way such answering may occur!) *it can be answered?*

Whoever is not prepared to concede that point will have to concern himself in a historical way with the self-consciousness of Jesus, and he will have to do so for theological reasons. That is, in fact, what is happening at present. Conzelmann has recently formulated that concern in this way, that "the question of Jesus' self-consciousness [has moved] to the very forefront of the whole attempt to reconstruct his teachings."[30]

If this effort is successful in achieving results, Jesus will become the point of origin for Christology in a different way than was the case with Bultmann. If, for Bultmann, Jesus' proclamation is the presupposition,

26. R. Bultmann, *Theology* (cited above, n. 6), I, 43.
27. *Ibid.,* pp. 9 f., 43.
28. R. Bultmann, "Zur Frage der Christologie" (cited above, n. 10), p. 101.
29. R. Bultmann, *Theology* (cited above, n. 6), I, 26.
30. Hans Conzelmann, "The Method of the Life-of-Jesus Research," in *The Historical Jesus* (cited above, n. 8), p. 64.

but not a part, of New Testament theology,[31] then actual theology begins only after Easter, with the explication of the implicit Christology. This new attempt can be characterized as one which concentrates on retaining the connection with what went before to the extent that it raises the question about the subject matter which becomes explicit. If this subject matter can be reached historically, it ought then to be included in theological reflection. In that case, New Testament theology would begin at an earlier point than it does with Bultmann. But how far can we go with such an approach?

Käsemann speaks of Jesus' "unparalleled and sovereign freedom," and says that Jesus undoubtedly "regarded himself as inspired." He maintains that Jesus must have understood himself "as the instrument of [the] living Spirit of God," even if Jesus did not use such words.[32] Bornkamm uses, among other words, the term "authority," in which is contained "the mystery of Jesus' personality and influence, as understood by faith." The word "authority" "denotes a reality which appertains to the historical Jesus and is prior to any interpretation. In his encounters with the most different people, Jesus' 'authority' is always immediately and authentically present."[33]

We must pause here, because, it seems to me, we must question whether it is not the case that several perspectives have been telescoped together in these sentences: the contingency of "authority"; the historical reality of that quality which is characterized as "authority," which belongs to Jesus prior to all interpretation; and the contingency of faith's interpretation of this reality as "authority." It is to be conceded that the reality to which the word "authority" points is not itself a derivable entity, in that the reports attempt no derivation (as an explicit Christology then later does). If, however, this reality belongs to Jesus *prior to all interpretation* (in that case, precisely, in fact, to the historical [*historisch*], and not the historic [*geschichtlich*], Jesus), then it is, nevertheless, historically comprehensible only through interpretation (which is, again, contingent), and hence in the designation by *faith* of this reality as "authority." This statement of faith (precisely because of its contingent character) certainly then goes beyond the simply "histori-

---

31. R. Bultmann, *Theology* (cited above, n. 6), I, 3.
32. E. Käsemann (cited above, n. 14), pp. 40–42.
33. G. Bornkamm, *Jesus of Nazareth* (cited above, n. 17), p. 60.

cal," but at the same time it blocks immediate access to the reality itself. And thus it is characteristic (and by no means an accident, but rather a necessity growing out of the subject matter itself) that Bornkamm, in connection with the sentences just quoted, develops the account of Jesus' authority in the light of passages which narrate the encounters various men had with Jesus.

The concept "authority" is thus already a christological interpretation, to be sure a christological interpretation *in nuce* to the extent that it does not yet make use of a title. The same thing can be said about Käsemann's characterization of Jesus' self-consciousness. That begins to become clear already in the fact that the terminology Käsemann uses ("sovereignty," "inspired," "instrument of the living Spirit of God") does not appear in the sources. The self-consciousness of Jesus is deduced from the proclamation which is regarded as authentic. This procedure cannot be questioned from a methodological standpoint. The only question concerns whether it is possible in this way to reach historical judgments about the self-consciousness of Jesus which are of sufficient certainty that the content, which at a later time became explicit in Christology, can already be presupposed in the historical Jesus.

We must therefore begin once more with the historical question. Let us bear in mind that the question concerning the self-consciousness of Jesus can be answered only by the historian. Let us further bear in mind that form criticism, through its demonstration of the nature of our sources, has rendered the possibility of a historical judgment so difficult that the necessary certainty cannot be achieved. In the light of that, I think, it is necessary to exercise somewhat more care.

Form criticism has taught us that the tradition has been shaped by faith for the purpose of proclamation. We have to do therefore with a tendentious shaping. But a tendency is *always* present. It would be present even in the kind of hypothetical case where the Christian community would have taken some stenographic records into its proclamation. The mere fact *that* the Christian community, which believed in Jesus, would call for faith in Jesus by means of such sayings of Jesus and would make use of such records means that these records were meaningful for its faith and for the expression of its faith. Records which could not do that, *could* not be accepted by the Christian community, even if they were historical. Therefore, even such possibly available records would be *used* tendentiously. For that very reason, it appears to me, historical elements (elements which are possibly historical) cannot be isolated by means of elimination, but rather (if at all, then) at most by means of interpretation. To put it another way, I am not able to differentiate between historical and tendentious elements. *Everything* is tendentious. The historical element has been screened by the tendency.

Historical elements, therefore, do not exist *prior* to what is christological. They cannot be found by seeking to bypass what is christological, but rather can be found only by going through what is christological, because Jesus is always confronted (even where his words alone are handed on) as the one who is announced from the perspective of faith. Thus even his "authority," his "sovereignty" are statements of one who believes.

A further observation must be included at this point. I will formulate it initially in this way: the church did not come into existence through Jesus *alone*. It appears to me that that is the element of truth to be found in Bultmann's understanding. Now Käsemann has rightly pointed out that the primitive Christian community, with its interest in the past, with its interest in Jesus, intends to show that "the *extra nos* of salvation is 'given' to faith."[34] We have already said that that does not have to happen with material which (according to *our* criteria and *our* judgment) is historical. Nothing historical is said in such a statement, however. Rather, what is indicated is simply a relationship to the past.

He who proclaims Jesus expresses in that act his relationship to Jesus, and at the same time he announces this relationship so that those who hear this proclamation will be taken into this relationship. This relationship exists in close connection to faith. Faith is (according to Ebeling's definition) "existence grounding itself in something outside itself."[35] Faith is therefore also a relationship.

Even if Jesus is prior to all faith, the one who believes makes his statements about Jesus only after he has entered into this relationship. This is what was intended with the sentence that the church did not come into existence through Jesus alone. The primal datum of the church is therefore not a person, but rather a relationship starting from this person. Thus Jesus and faith belong together. To put it more exactly, we

---

34. E. Käsemann (cited above, n. 14), p. 33. ["*Extra nos*" is a Latin phrase, meaning "outside us," which refers to that aspect of salvation which is beyond the subjective existence of the believer; it is contrasted with "*in nos*," which means "in (or within) us" and expresses the subjective element of the Christian faith. —TRANSLATOR.]

35. Gerhard Ebeling, *Was Heisst Glauben?* (Tübingen: J. C. B. Mohr, 1958), p. 15.

would have to say that Jesus and the one who believes belong together. They are bound together by a relationship. At this point, we may leave as an open question whether this relationship is itself already the relationship of faith, or whether we have to do here with a relationship which only makes faith possible, which leads to faith. We will have to occupy ourselves with this question later on.

In any case, however, it must be stated (and at this point form criticism is brought to bear) that this relationship between the one who believes and Jesus can be grasped by *us* only at one of its poles, namely, at the point where men state this relationship. But when they state this relationship, they interpret Jesus, implicitly or explicitly. It could be put in the following way: by means of this interpretation, the statement, which has its interest in faith, *captures* the historical Jesus. The picture of Jesus which now arises *cannot* any longer be a purely historical picture, even though it *intends* to present the historical Jesus. This mingling of the one in the other presented no difficulty to men in that period, because they gave their reports as those who *believed*, but did not make objective presentations, and because they were not aware of the historical question.

At this point it also becomes clear why the alternative "continuity or discontinuity" is problematical. It is possible to speak of continuity or discontinuity only if historical judgments are made, and then the "historical Jesus" is compared with the Jesus who is proclaimed by those witnesses who stand in a relationship to him. The relationship would thus have to be dissolved. But are there statements about Jesus which exist apart from this relationship? Therefore, we simply cannot set up this sequence of "historical Jesus/witnesses to him," which alone would make possible a judgment concerning continuity or discontinuity. Rather, our statements show just the opposite movement. The witnesses (who are always later than Jesus) make statements about Jesus (who is therefore the earlier one).

This means—and with this observation we reach the end of our preliminary methodological considerations—that the beginning of Christology cannot be defined in such a way that a decision must be made either for the primitive Christian community or for the historical Jesus. Rather, the beginnings lie at the point where the relationship between Jesus and the believer becomes visible for the first time. We shall attempt to reach this point from three directions in the discussion that follows.

Jesus and the
Son of Man

When we turn to the text, it is clear from our preliminary considerations that we cannot simply ask what Jesus' preaching was like, or what his acts were like. Rather we must always allow these questions to remain within a framework that takes seriously the results of form criticism. We can therefore only ask how did the primitive community present him whom they proclaimed as one who acted? How did the primitive community present him whom they proclaimed as one who proclaimed? How did the primitive community present Jesus himself, the one whom they proclaimed?

If we begin with the last question, we must investigate the titles given to Jesus. The primitive community attributed titles and honorifics to Jesus and expressed in that way that he whom they proclaimed was the one in whom they believed. I cannot go into all such titles attributed to Jesus, and have no need to, since many of them are without doubt secondary. They arise only at a later time.

There is nevertheless an interesting group of titles in the older strata of the tradition: Jesus is designated as rabbi, as teacher, as prophet. Naturally, the element of *honorific* title plays a part here as well. "Rabbi" (my master) was a title of honor for prominent teachers of the law. "The prophet" (with the article emphasized) can be a title for an eschatological figure. I would like to point to something else however. It is quite significant that by means of these titles the function of proclamation is always in some way expressed. It is precisely at that point that the interest of the community is apparently to be found. The one whom they proclaim is himself presented as one who proclaims.

The fact *that* Jesus preached can scarcely be doubted. But when the element of his preaching is bound up with such a title, the one who proclaims is then qualified by the proclamation. From the preaching, its content or the way in which it is carried out, an inference is made concerning the authority of the one who preaches. Already at this point the way is prepared for the transition from implicit to explicit Christology.

We must first, however, continue our examination, and observe the content of this proclamation. At this point, a further element comes into view. Within the varied content of the proclamation we are met with a further title, "Son of man." But one thing is striking. With only four exceptions, the title Son of man is found in the New Testament solely in the Gospels, and there only in the mouth of Jesus.

The situation, therefore, is such that the primitive community presents the one proclaimed as the proclaimer, whereby the content of the proclamation is precisely a title. The question that now arises is this: in what relationship does the proclaimer of the title stand (in the presentation of the primitive community) to the title itself?

Now there is no doubt at all that at least the evangelists have applied this title to Jesus. But that is by no means a foregone conclusion, because (even in the presentation of the Gospel writers) the proclaimer, Jesus, never applies this title to himself in so many words. Rather, he speaks without exception of the Son of man in the third person. The question thus arises whether the evangelists have interpreted correctly when they transfer this title to Jesus.

To answer this we must investigate the sources. The findings indicate that the title appears in the whole range of the tradition, in "Q," Mark, and in the special sources of Matthew and Luke. To be sure, even a cursory glance indicates that the concept of Son of man is used in a wide variety of ways. Bultmann has worked out three groups which can be clearly differentiated from one another.[36] Jesus speaks (1) of the coming Son of man, (2) the Son of man who suffers and is raised from the dead, and (3) of the Son of man who is acting at the present moment. Let us look briefly at these three groups.

(1) Jesus speaks of the coming Son of man. That occurs for the most part in an apocalyptic sense. That implies as the lightning flashes, he will be there. That implies, keep yourself ready now for his hour. In this sense (always as the announcement of another) the title appears in the following places, among others: Mark 13:26; 14:62; Matthew 24:27, 37, 39, 44; Luke 12:40; 17:24, 26.

If this were the only group we had, it would be a fairly simple matter.

36. R. Bultmann, *The History of the Synoptic Tradition* (cited above, n. 12), cf. "General Index"; *Theology* (cited above, n. 6), I, 30.

The title Son of man would have to be eliminated as a title for Jesus. At most, one would then have to investigate whether the community had nevertheless understood this as a title for Jesus at a later time. For that, however, one could find no support from the sources. There is no preparation in them for the transference of the title to Jesus.

(2) Jesus speaks of the Son of man who suffers and is raised from the dead. This group is absent in "Q." It appears for the first time in Mark (8:31; 9:9, 12, 31; 10:33, 45, and where they exist, in the Synoptic parallels).

These sayings about the Son of man are absolutely incompatible with those of the first group. Those in the first group concern the *Parousia* of the Son of man, those in the second group his suffering, death, and *resurrection*.

There is no point in trying to harmonize these two groups, although it must be admitted that such harmonization is apparently quite possible. The second group needs only to be placed before the first group, and the result is a neat succession of events in "salvation-history." The second group says that the Son of man will suffer, die, and rise again (and there is no doubt that Jesus is meant here). The first group says that he will return at the Parousia (and *then* Jesus would also be meant here).

But this harmonizing cannot be undertaken for the following reasons. *First,* these two motifs (dying/rising and Parousia) never appear together. Yet if originally both of these are supposed to have been said of Jesus, it would be quite strange that at times only the first, at other times only the second, motif would be mentioned. *Secondly,* it must be observed that from a literary standpoint the second group is more recent. It does not confront us until Mark. These sayings about the Son of man presume a knowledge of the events of the Passion and Easter, at times down to the very details. *Thirdly,* it must be pointed out that the first group can be explained in connection with the apocalypticism of late Judaism. (We will return to this matter later on.) This is not the case with the second group, however, since suffering — dying — rising have no parallel in the presentation of the Son of man found in Jewish apocalyptic thinking.

That means, however, that in this second group nothing has been taken over except the concept, nothing except the title. Earlier contents have been detached from the concept. This concept has then been filled with a new content taken from the event of Jesus. If we view this from the perspective of Mark, in whose work this second group confronts us for the first time, that group speaks not of a Son of man who is coming, but of a Son of man who is already present.

Despite this great difference from the sayings about the Son of man contained in the first group, which has up to now shown itself to be the earlier, it is noteworthy that the "style" of that group has been retained. In the second group also the Son-of-man sayings appear only in the mouth of Jesus and only in the third person.

(3) Jesus speaks of the Son of man at work in the present. This group of sayings is not very extensive in terms of numbers, and is quite heterogeneous. The Son of man has authority to forgive sins (Mark 2:10); he is Lord even of the Sabbath (Mark 2:28); he has no place where he may lay his head (Matt. 8:20); he has come, he eats and drinks, and people say that he is a glutton and a drunkard and is the companion of tax collectors and sinners (Matt. 11:19 par.; 12:32 par.), etc. This group appears, if only sporadically, in all strata of tradition.

It is tempting to conclude that these sayings developed out of the sayings contained in the second group. If Jesus who suffers dies and rises again is designated in those sayings as Son of man, then here he is the one who has come and is at work, for it is also quite certain that Jesus is also meant in these statements (despite the third person). But such a development is nonetheless unlikely. The wide dissemination of the sayings in the third group indicates rather that they are older and that out of them Mark has created the sayings of the second group.

The opinion has been rather widely represented that "Son of man" is used in group three not in any titular sense, but represents rather a slavish translation from the Aramaic, where it stood for "man" or "I."[37] If that is valid, the entire group can be dismissed from our considerations. To be sure, that is not at all certain — at least not for all the passages. The influence of the community upon the formation of the tradition will certainly have to be taken into consideration.[38] But in that case, it is further evident that the term Son of man is virtually nothing

37. Cf. among others Julius Wellhausen, *Einleitung in die drei ersten Evangelien* (Berlin: Reimer, ²1911), pp. 128 ff.; R. Bultmann, *Theology* (cited above, n. 6), I, 30.

38. Thus Erik K. T. Sjöberg *Der verborgene Menschensohn in den Evangelien* (Lund: C. W. K. Gleerup, 1955), p. 239; cf. also G. Bornkamm, *Jesus of Nazareth* (cited above, n. 17), pp. 229 f.

but a cipher. The content with which the term is filled comes from the Jesus-tradition.

Now, it is possible once more to attempt a harmonizing. But the same objections which I mentioned above, also confront us here. We have, therefore, this peculiar finding, namely, that the three groups of sayings about the Son of man are related only through this same concept. The contents differ, and in no instance do even two of the content groups appear together. Two possible explanations suggest themselves here.

First, it is conceivable that we have to do here with competing traditions. In that case the three groups would have arisen alongside one another, perhaps in different circles within the community, perhaps in different places. But this possibility is quite unlikely, since the second group, at least, was shown to be secondary from a literary standpoint.

In that case, however, we would have to assume that the groups did not stand alongside one another competitively, but rather that they arose one after another, the first group (as I already indicated) being the oldest.

Here it is again possible to recognize a course of development. The Son-of-man concept, which originally pointed to the future, is at a later time related also to the past. If the primitive community presents Jesus' preaching in the first instance in such a way that he announced the coming Son of man, it later also presented his preaching in such a way that Jesus spoke of a Son of man who came, who was at work, and who suffered, died, and rose from the dead. In that way the Son-of-man concept was filled with what the community handed on concerning Jesus and his fate. The title now served the christological interpretation of Jesus. This development then continued further, as can be seen in Matthew. The title becomes practically a name. Thus, Matthew can employ the personal pronoun (16:21) at a point where his source speaks of the Son of man (Mark 9:31); but also, on the contrary, he can speak of the Son of man (16:13) where there is a personal pronoun in the source (Mark 8:27).

Having thus caught sight of a course of development, we must now go back a step; we then find ourselves confronted with the question of how things stand with regard to the first group of Son-of-man sayings. What was the community's understanding when it had Jesus announce the coming Son of man?

But is the question at all correctly put? Is the coming Son of man really proclaimed here? To formulate it another way, does this proclamation really look to the future? Attention must be paid here to the difference between apocalyptic proclamation in late Judaism and the proclamation of Jesus in the presentation of the primitive community. The title Son of man confronts us for the first time, so far as the term is concerned, in Daniel 7. It is certainly very questionable whether an individual figure is intended in this passage, whether we are not on the contrary to think in this instance of "something like the figure of a man" (in contrast to the four beasts), that is, to think of a symbolic figure, which incorporates the heavenly kingdom in contrast to the human kingdoms.[39] Individualization occurs only later. In IV Ezra [II Esdras] 13 the Son of man is the judge of the nations and the redeemer of Israel. He is here almost a political-messianic figure. In the "Parables" of the Ethiopic Enoch (I Enoch 37-71) the Son of man is something like a forerunner of the kingdom. He is judge, revealer, he is also active in the kingdom—but he does not bring it. The kingdom is brought by God himself.

The various conceptions of the Son of man which circulated shortly before, or at the time of, the New Testament cannot be brought into one systematic picture. The only thing they all have in common is that they are oriented to the future, and they portray the picture of the future in colors and features which are in part quite fanciful. Here what is announced is really the *future,* in which the Son of man (along with other figures) is also to play a role.

Now there can be no doubt that these ideas have influenced the first group of New Testament sayings about the Son of man. The only question concerns the actual extent of such influence. It cannot be determined exactly to which of the various ideas of the Son of man reference is made. The question can be raised whether any *one* particular idea must be assumed at all. Perhaps the only important point is that the Son of man is a figure of the future. In any case, this is the element that binds the first group to late Jewish apocalypticism. To be sure, certain differentiations must also be made here, as we shall see in a moment. In order to determine them, we must again proceed from findings and trace backward the history of the tradition.

First of all, it is certain that the community identified the coming Son

39. Cf. Philipp Vielhauer, "Gottesreich und Menschensohn in der Verkündigung Jesu," in *Festschrift für Günther Dehn* (Neukirchen: Verlag der Buchhandlung des Erziehungsvereins, 1957), pp. 71 ff., reprinted in Vielhauer's *Aufsätze zum Neuen Testament* ("Theologische Bücherei," 31 [Munich: Chr. Kaiser Verlag, 1965]), pp. 79 ff.

of man with Jesus. The apocalyptic passages in the Synoptics demon-
strate that with all the clarity we could want. But did the community
make this identification from the very beginning? There have been
those (Julius Wellhausen, Rudolf Bultmann, and others) who represent
the view that this first group of sayings contains (at least in part) authentic proclamation by Jesus; in this view, it must also be noted, however, Jesus did not announce his own imminent coming, but rather the
coming of another, because, so this view holds, Jesus clearly speaks of
the Son of man in the third person.

But is this reason compelling? In the second and third groups of the
Son-of-man sayings, identification of this figure with Jesus is, despite the
use of the third person which is also employed there, certainly carried
through. Is it then impossible in the first group?

To be sure, a presupposition would have to be made here. It would
have to be assumed that the title "Son of man" had already been transferred to Jesus before this first group of sayings arose. But the first group
would also share such a presupposition with the second and the third,
and for the present it is still an open question where that transference
took place. But let us make this presupposition at this point, and let us
presuppose at the same time that the community was awaiting the
Parousia of Jesus (something which is the case, for example, with Paul,
quite apart from any idea of the Son of man). In that case, something
could have happened in the first group of sayings comparable to that
which happened in the second and third groups. The existing identification of Jesus with the Son of man, a titular and therefore purely
formal identification, was filled with what was being proclaimed about
Jesus, namely, his Parousia. Thus we would have to do here (to be sure,
always on the basis of the presupposition mentioned above) with later
formulations of the community.

Two questions now remain open, both of which belong together.
(1) Are there any indications at all that the transference of the title Son
of man to Jesus is preceded by a stage in the tradition which knows of
the Son-of-man title, but which unquestionably and clearly does not
(not *yet*) designate Jesus by it? And, if this question is to be answered
affirmatively, (2) is there any way to explain how the point was reached
where this transference took place, a transference that clearly and unquestionably dominates the tradition at a later time?

The first question is to be answered, in my opinion, in the affirmative. We must at this point investigate a group of Son-of-man sayings contained within the first group, sayings which are distinguished from the other sayings in this group by the fact that they are not exclusively oriented to the future (and are thus not simply to be designated as apocalyptic), but rather also have an element of the present in them. This group is to be found both in Mark and in "Q."

Mark 8:38: "For whoever is ashamed of me and of my words in this adulterous and sinful generation, of him will the Son of man also be ashamed, when he comes in the glory of his Father with the holy angels." Similarly Luke 12:8 f.: "And I tell you, everyone who acknowledges me before men, the Son of man also will acknowledge before the angels of God, but he who denies me before men will be denied before the angels of God."

It can be assumed that both of these sayings have a common root, which has been altered in different ways. In the Marcan form, the Son of man is conceived as more than a judge. In the Lucan form the angels have the function of judgment; the Son of man appears as counsel. The idea of the Son of man is thus not uniform. Against the background of this difference, however, the element which they do have in common becomes clear, and because of this element these sayings stand out from the framework of the remaining sayings of the first group. In these two sayings, Jesus and the Son of man are *explicitly* distinguished from one another (not simply by means of the use of the third person!). The relationship between the two consists in the fact that the coming Son of man will judge or acknowledge men according to their present conduct toward Jesus.

Now, is this saying old? This question will have to be answered with an unqualified affirmative, because it hardly appears imaginable that such a saying could have arisen after the title "Son of man" had already been transferred to Jesus. This transference is thus shown to be secondary. This can also be shown indirectly in terms of the tradition history of this saying, since it is clear that this saying would have to cause difficulties for the later community (precisely because of the distinction between Jesus and the Son of man).

I have already noted that Luke had the "Q" form of the saying as his source. The parallels in Matthew indicate that. In Matthew it is formulated in one instance in this way (10:32 f.), "So every one who acknowledges me before men, *I* also will acknowledge before my Father who is in heaven; but whoever denies me before men, *I* also will deny before my Father who is in heaven." The other form reads (16:27): "For the Son of man is to come with his angels in the glory of his Father, and then he will repay every man *for what he has done.*" In both instances the difficulties have been set aside. In the first instance it is accomplished by putting the personal pronoun "I" in place of the term "Son of man" for Jesus, something which, as we have already seen, is characteristic of Matthew. In the second instance the judgment is carried out, not according to the conduct toward Jesus, but according to what a man has done. Thus Jesus is eliminated in the first part of the saying, and in that way there is opened up the possibility of understanding Jesus as the Son of man who judges.

Therefore, the Marcan and Lucan formulations of the saying may well be older from the point of view of tradition history, since both of them still distinguish between Jesus and the Son of man, and thereby contradict the later formulation. If we compare Mark and Luke with one another, it is apparently possible to ascertain a development here as well. For this we are concerned not so much with the second half of the saying as we are with the first half. Mark formulates it in this way: "whoever is ashamed of me and my words . . ."; Luke, on the contrary, "whoever acknowledges me before men. . . ." Now it is precisely the changes in Matthew which indicate that the longer the tradition exists, the more the *person* of Jesus is singled out and moved more emphatically toward the center. If we assume the presence of this tendency here as well, then Luke displays a more developed form compared to Mark. He speaks of acknowledging Jesus, without including reference to the words of Jesus as Mark still does. When this is seen, it is possible to pose the question whether it is not the case that the following development in the tradition is evident: (1) "Whoever is ashamed of *my words* . . ."; (2) "Whoever is ashamed of *me* and my words . . ."; (3) "Whoever acknowledges *me* before men. . . ."

It is customary at this point to ask whether we have to do in the oldest stage of the tradition with words of the historical Jesus. If this is affirmed,[40] it is apparently possible in the discussion of the origins of Christology to differentiate neatly in following way: Jesus proclaims the coming of the Son of man; the community then identified him with the

40. Thus, among others, G. Bornkamm, *Jesus of Nazareth* (cited above, n. 17), p. 228.

one who comes. But there are still objections to be noted here, indeed even apart from any historical verdict. I have already pointed to the basic difficulties. Time and again arguments, eminently worthy of consideration, have been brought forward against the authenticity of this saying.[41] The verdict therefore remains unsure. But above all, is it really possible here to differentiate so neatly between Jesus and the community? Even if these words were historical, it can nevertheless not be disputed that it was the *early primitive community* which handed on sayings of Jesus in which he spoke of the coming Son of man without identifying himself even implicitly with that figure. There was therefore in any case in the primitive community a stage in the tradition in which the Son of man had not yet been identified with Jesus. If we express this in a more general way, and make use of terminology we used earlier, we could formulate it provisionally in this manner: there was in the *primitive community* a stage in the tradition in which the one who was proclaimed had not yet in express words, and therefore not unequivocally, appeared as the one proclaimed, but rather as the one who proclaimed.

Now what does that mean for the beginnings of Christology? We pursue this problem when we take up once again the question which I posed earlier, namely, can we really say that the primitive community has Jesus here proclaim the coming Son of man? That would only be the case if this saying were interested in the *future* (as later the apocalyptic sayings then are). But in this instance the purpose is not at all to instruct about the future. Indeed, the statements about the future lack uniformity, because they employ different conceptions of the Son of man. The only thing which is assumed is *that* the Son of man is coming, however this may be conceived.

In our saying, on the other hand, the emphasis lies upon the way in which someone reacts to Jesus' words or to himself *now*. It is therefore completely oriented to, and interested in, the present. The reaction to Jesus' words or to himself is qualified. This qualification occurs, to be sure, against the background of eschatological expectation. But the

---

41. Cf., among others, E. Käsemann, "Sätze heiligen Rechtes im Neuen Testament," *New Testament Studies*, 1 (1954–55), pp. 256 ff., reprinted in *Exegetische Versuche und Besinnungen*, II (Göttingen: Vandenhoeck & Ruprecht, 1964), pp. 78 ff.; Eng. trans. "Sentences of Holy Law in the New Testament," in *New Testament Questions of Today*, trans. W. J. Montague (Philadelphia: Fortress, 1969), pp. 77–78. By the same author, "Problem of the Historical Jesus," in *Essays* (cited above, n. 14), pp. 43 f.; P. Vielhauer (cited above, n. 39), pp. 68 ff. (*Aufsätze*, pp. 76 ff.).

important point is not this expectation, but rather it is said that the
reaction to Jesus' words, and to Jesus, has eschatological consequences.

And precisely here we have to do with the beginnings of Christology.
Here we encounter the relationship about which I spoke at the conclusion of the preliminary methodological considerations. But this relationship is one which is qualified eschatologically, and therefore *the
eschatological element is the primal datum of Christology.*

It is customary today to differentiate between implicit and explicit
(or between indirect and direct) Christology. An explicit (or direct)
Christology is evident only when honorific titles and the like are transferred to Jesus. It is possible to carry through this differentiation, but it
ought to be recognized that it is a loaded differentiation. It expresses a
leap, namely, from proclaimer to one proclaimed, and then in addition
the claim is made that it is possible to speak of actual Christian preaching only at the point where the proclaimer has become the one proclaimed.[42]

The christological element (and indeed, "christological" in the fullest
sense) which is provided with the proclaimer and his proclamation
thereby either recedes to an inadmissible degree or disappears entirely.
It is correct that the proclaimer is not yet the one who is believed in (not
in the latter meaning of the term). "I believe *in* Jesus Christ" is a later
statement. And yet Jesus and his proclamation are not without any
connection to faith. If we examine this saying more closely, we see that
we are dealing with *two relationships.* The one binds Jesus and his proclamation to man, the other binds man with the coming Son of man,
with the future, with the judgment which is indeed the judgment of
God. It is helpful, initially, to distinguish between these two relationships, even though it is clear that they are not to be separated, that
indeed there was an interest in combining them.

It is important for a person to survive the judgment, to enter into
God's kingdom, and now he is told that this decision concerning his
future has been anticipated. It occurs in the first relationship, it occurs
in the reaction of the person to Jesus and his proclamation. In just that
way the relationship is qualified as an eschatological one. The *entire*
relationship is Christology.

But it then also becomes clear that *this* Christology always expresses
more than every so-called explicit Christology. For what happens in the

42. R. Bultmann, *Primitive Christianity* (cited above, n. 7), p. 93.

course of becoming explicit? *One* pole of this relationship is interpreted. For the purpose of interpretation, reference is made to familiar material which is offered by tradition and environment.

In that way, however, the immediacy which was originally present is lost. No title can express this immediacy at a later time—not even the sum total of all titles can do it. But we can understand how titles then came to be transferred to Jesus.

The early primitive community described it thus: Jesus demands a relationship to himself and to his words, a relationship which he qualifies as an eschatological one. People who have experienced it in its immediacy give it expression. They desire in this way to present it to others who do not yet stand in this relationship, but whom they would gladly bring into it. But then they confront the task of explaining to these other people the necessity of such a relationship. And that happens precisely through interpreting Jesus. But with that the condition is present for Jesus to be given expression also independently of the relationship. The eschatological element of the original immediacy is objectified in a title. Nevertheless the aim is not really to qualify Jesus, not to qualify his person; rather the title has, as it were, a potential function. It is intended to establish, and thereby keep open, the possibility of a new eschatological relationship. That a doctrine of the person of Jesus arose as the separation became greater is a development that is all too easy to understand, a development which then becomes a part of the history of doctrine.

But if we now look in the opposite direction, we can perhaps venture the conjecture that our saying about the Son of man goes back to the pre-Easter period precisely because of the immediacy that is expressed in it. Again, I do not maintain that it is historical. But this saying is nevertheless a saying that comes from a point very close to historicity.

Before I undertake some concluding considerations on the transference of the title Son of man to Jesus, I should like very briefly to inquire at one point into the relationship between "Son of man" and the term *basileia*.[43] Philipp Vielhauer, in an article in the *Festschrift* for Günther Dehn to which I have already referred, has pointed to a discrepancy which exists here. These two ideas are not connected in Jewish apocalyptic. Synoptic findings show that there too they belong consistently to

43. [Greek word meaning "kingdom" which is used in the phrase "kingdom of God."
—TRANSLATOR.]

different strata of tradition. Vielhauer contends that Jesus (and indeed the historical Jesus) made the kingdom of God the central subject of his proclamation, and that the expectation of a Son of man has no place within it.

Now we have on principle avoided any historical judgment. For that reason, the problem confronts us in slightly different form. There is no doubt that both traditions appear in the early primitive community, if not connected to one another, at least side by side. But is it understandable, when such a discrepancy exists?

We must pose the question for the third time: is it really a matter of the proclamation of the future? Is it a matter of instruction about future things? We have already seen that even in the oldest forms of the sayings about the Son of man, the *representations* of the future have not been brought into agreement. It is much rather the case that—with the aid of the material concerning the future—the present, the relationship to Jesus, is qualified eschatologically.

For that reason no real discrepancy with the sayings about the kingdom exists. To be sure, apocalyptic elements and motifs are encountered there in the later traditions too. But they are not present at the beginning. Neither the question about the "how" nor the question about the "when" plays any part. But in just this way the peculiarity of the sayings about the kingdom is indicated and, indeed, in a way that corresponds exactly to that which we have just established concerning the sayings about the Son of man. They do not exist for themselves, but rather they serve the eschatological qualification of the relationship to Jesus. The questions about the "when" and the "how" are, as Conzelmann has expressed it, surpassed. As long as questions are still put with any apocalyptic interest at all, the appeal has not yet even been understood.[44]

From this point we can now also understand how it can be said that time has come to an end. There *is* in fact *no* more time. It is a matter of an *immediate metanoia,* of an immediate *pistis* (cf. Mark 1:15).[45] The

44. H. Conzelmann, "Gegenwart und Zukunft in der synoptischen Tradition," in *Zeitschrift für Theologie und Kirche,* 55 (1957), 287; Eng. trans. "Present and Future in the Synoptic Tradition," trans. Jack Wilson, in *God and Christ: Existence and Province,* Journal for Theology and the Church 5 (Tübingen: J. C. B. Mohr, New York: Harper & Row, 1968), p. 36.

45. [*Metanoia* is a Greek word usually translated as "repentance." It means to undergo a change (*meta*) in thinking (*noia*). *Pistis* is a Greek word which means "faith" or "trust." —TRANSLATOR.]

primitive community understood the proclamation of the kingdom in such a way that a person in confrontation with Jesus must decide *now* for or against him. Because the kingdom is near, because the Son of man is coming, because the eschaton is at the very gates, repentance and faith are offered in Jesus.

Jesus thus brings the eschatological moment, in that in the relationship to him the eschatological judgment is anticipated. When we have seen this, we can recognize that we already have here what Paul later worked out in his proclamation about justification as "something that had already taken place." But that is not yet explicit here, indeed it cannot be at all explicit, since the encounter with Jesus is an unmediated one. It is not until this encounter is *articulated* that a beginning is made at working out this relationship. But these words (including Paul's words about justification) always say less than the contents itself, because they place the contents within the framework of a specific representation, a prior conceptuality.

We want at this point to ask how it came about that the title "Son of man" was transferred to Jesus. To be sure, we have already touched on this problem, but we must now give consideration to some specific points, since the transference of the title occurs in a twofold way.

The first way is present in the second and third groups of the Son-of-man sayings. We could say that we have here an almost normal christological development. What had happened in an unmediated relationship to Jesus is worked out by Christians who had themselves not participated in such a relationship. On Jesus, who serves as one pole of this relationship, is bestowed some particular qualification. As elsewhere, this is done by giving him a title. Jesus is called the Christ, the Son of God—and here, it is the title of Son of man which is conferred upon him. But what is remarkable here is the fact that this concept has completely lost its content. Traditionally, the Son of man is the one who comes. Here, however, he is the one who has come, or more exactly, one who has already come. This title which indicates the future has been filled with material drawn from the past, with the deeds (third group), with the suffering, dying, and rising of Jesus (second group). As a result, it could be said to the Jewish environment: the Son of man for whom you wait has already appeared. And if the Son of man is traditionally the one who begins the final events, then the fact that he has appeared means that the final period of time has already begun—admittedly, in another way than it had been expected.

In addition, however, the title "Son of man" is transferred to Jesus in the sense that it expresses his coming (or his coming again). That occurs in the first group of the sayings about the Son of man (with the exception of those that are related to the present).

Which of these two ways of transference for the title is the older? We can omit the second group of sayings at this point, because we do not meet it until the Gospel of Mark; in that way it is proven to be more recent. The decision is therefore between the first and the third groups. Was the title "Son of man" first transferred to Jesus because he was awaited as the one who was to come? Or was it transferred in order to give expression to the belief that he who was otherwise awaited as the one who was to come, had already appeared? Arguments can be advanced for both positions.

At first glance, the most attractive conjecture would be that the title was transferred in its futuristic meaning. Since the future is decided in terms of relationship to Jesus, Jesus is precisely identical with the one by whom the future is decided at the time of judgment. If the title was transferred in that way, it is filled out with material concerning Jesus.

In that case it is, to be sure, somewhat astonishing that there is no instance in the third group where the coming Son of man is spoken of. The idea of Jesus' coming (or coming again) was not given up again, once it had arisen.

Are we then to assume a development in reverse order? In that case only the title (and nothing else) was first transferred to Jesus (third group). The Son of man *was* already there, and then, from the title, the thought was developed that Jesus was *also* expected as the coming Son of man.

But perhaps it is not a matter of an alternative at all. The transference of the title "Son of man" to Jesus must certainly have occurred against the background of the oldest layer of tradition. The futuristic relationship was used as an eschatological qualification of the relationship between Jesus and man. In this way the futuristic element was inserted into this relationship. If Jesus was then designated as Son of man, he would be Son of man both as the one who is to come as well as the one who has already been present. Both groups, the first and the third, thus come from the same root. Neither is immediately dependent on the other.

Is it now possible to determine when this transference took place? A look at Paul shows us that the expectation of the Parousia of Jesus (even

without employment of the title Son of man) is very old. Can it already
have been present before Easter?

The fact that the testimony we have is later than Easter does not immediately speak against that possibility. The testimony could have
preserved older material. Nevertheless it is quite significant that the
early primitive community handed on traditions *after* Easter which
speak of the approaching kingdom; or, to put it more carefully, traditions which still *also* speak of the approaching kingdom, whose advent
some still expect to experience (Mark 9:1). Is such a tradition likely to
have arisen in the primitive community if, already prior to Easter, expectation concerning the future was bound up with the coming of
Jesus?

It appears to me that another consideration is still more important.
How could the expectation of the coming of Jesus have been imagined
at all, prior to Easter? One would have to have known either that Jesus
would die and then *arise* and come again *later,* or that he would die and
then come again at the *Parousia.*

Now it is, of course, not impossible that Jesus and his followers reckoned with his death. But very little can be determined about that. The
predictions of Jesus' suffering and resurrection are all secondary. That
can be demonstrated by means of literary criticism. The Easter events
also indicate this in an indirect manner, since they present the resurrection as something which was astonishing. When the subject of Jesus'
suffering and death was spoken of *after* Easter, it could be treated in no
other way than that knowledge of the resurrection was attached to it.

Only, how could one combine expectation of the Parousia with the
death of Jesus *prior to* Easter, even if one reckoned with his death? That
could occur only if there was a desire to make statements about *Jesus'*
future by means of apocalyptic terminology. But in that case, the point
which just confronted us in the sayings about the Son of man (and the
basileia) would not have been taken seriously, namely, the urgency,
which surpassed the question about the "when" and the "how" of the
future. Only by ignoring that could anyone have been interested in an
apocalyptic timetable: Jesus will suffer, die, arise, come at the Parousia.
And then it would be possible to think about an interim period, and
about the duration and the meaning of this interim between resurrection and Parousia.

The heterogeneity of the representations of the future, however,
argues against all that. The future as such is not discussed at all, rather

the relationship to Jesus is qualified as an eschatological one by means of these representations of the future.

The person who stands in this relationship already stands in a relationship that is significant for the coming kingdom. But that is possible in its immediacy only for so long a time as Jesus is present. After his death the aspect shifts. The immediacy is no longer at hand. The relationship which is significant for the coming kingdom is in the past. But the kingdom is still to come. And so men live in the interim.

The origin of the expectation of Jesus' Parousia must therefore probably be placed in this period. At this point the idea of the Son of man offered assistance. It is possible, although this can be nothing more than a conjecture, that Easter itself provided the bridge from expectation of the Son of man or of the kingdom, to expectation of the Parousia of Jesus.

Let us compare in this light the ideas about the Son of man with those concerning the risen one. The Son of man in apocalyptic thinking is a preexistent, heavenly being. He is hidden with God, or he is being "held back" by God until his time comes. Now it is difficult to get at what the oldest Easter kerygma expresses through the simple verb form *ōphthē*.[46] In the New Testament itself it occurs subsequently in various ways: he allowed himself to be seen, he appeared—all the way to the expanded reports of the appearances of the risen Jesus.

But it is always a matter of an *apokalypsis* (a "revealing"), a stepping out from hiddenness. It is a breaking into this world from outside of it, and is therefore an eschatological event. What is significant in this *apokalypsis* is the fact that it occurs to or in a person who can be and is identified with the one who was crucified. There is therefore a certain parallel in this "mode of appearance," as it can be called, to the ideas about the Son of man.

The breaking in of the eschaton (in this instance, in seeing the risen one) means the end of time, but this end of time immediately becomes a past event. Time goes on, the world in which man lives continues to exist, and it remains visibly the same world as previously. Thus the tension arises between the event of the inbreaking of the eschaton in the

---

46. [This is a passive form, in the past ("aorist") tense, of the Greek verb *horaō*, "to see." It is used in I Cor. 15:5–8 and in I Tim. 3:16 with the dative case, in such a way as to make it difficult to determine whether it means "was seen by" or "appeared to." —TRANSLATOR.]

encounter with Jesus and with the risen one *on the one hand,* and the coming which continues to remain a future event *on the other.*

Nevertheless, the kingdom, the eschaton, is now no longer *exclusively* expectation. The *beginning* of the kingdom lies in the past—to be sure, not in such a way that the kingdom had already come and now continues, but nevertheless in such a way that one knows of a beginning in the past. This beginning is not presented as "kingdom," as a present condition, as a renewed world, but rather as the relationship to a person.

The situation is therefore this: the kingdom *has* (already) broken in (once) in the relationship to a *person, and* the kingdom is expected. But if the kingdom is present in the encounter with a person, then it does not require much of a step to place this person in the midst of the expected kingdom also. The relationship to the future is now also represented as a relationship to a person, and in just that way the transference of the title "Son of man" to this person is close at hand.

It is, therefore, not surprising that the coming *basileia* can continue to be spoken of even after Easter, and that both ideas (the Parousia of Jesus as the Son of man, and the coming of the kingdom) circulate side by side, since the element of urgency is bound up with both of these motifs. But because the coming kingdom is then interpreted in a new way and receives, with the expectation of Jesus' coming, a new center, the element of urgency now adheres primarily to Jesus.

And now the circle is closed. This urgency has its roots already in Jesus' eschatological proclamation, as the primitive community handed it on in the early sayings about the Son of man. Bultmann once put it in the following manner in a discussion: Jesus disregards time. That seems to me to be a good formulation, if, as Conzelmann has remarked, one understands the concept of "disregarding" as a positive qualification.[47] This "disregarding" means that there is no more time, because the future judgment has been anticipated in the eschatologically qualified relationship to Jesus.

But if then people know, also after Easter, that they are in the last times, then they express it in such a way that the *one who will come* is Jesus. In this way, then, the proclamation of the tradition about Jesus

47. H. Conzelmann, "Gegenwart und Zukunft in der synoptischen Tradition" (cited above, n. 44), p. 288, n. 2; Eng. trans. "Present and Future in the Synoptic Tradition," p. 37, n. 42.

can be qualified eschatologically after Easter by the idea of the expected
Parousia of Jesus, just as before Easter the relationship to Jesus was
qualified eschatologically by the ideas about the future.

In that case, however, it is necessary to bear in mind that the idea of
Jesus as the coming Son of man dare not be understood apocalyptically
(at least not at the beginning). When the early post-Easter community
speaks of the coming kingdom and of the Parousia of Jesus as the Son of
man, *it, too,* does not do that in order to give instruction in apocalyptic
matters. That is shown most clearly in Paul, who also seems to have
been the first to have taken up the concept of *parousia* in Christian
thought.

The case is the same here as it was earlier in the proclamation of the
basileia, namely, that the chief concern does not center on the "when"
and the "how," but rather on the urgency. And when Jesus is now proclaimed as the coming Son of man, the same urgency is retained which
had been provided through the presence of Jesus prior to Easter.

We could formulate the matter in a somewhat exaggerated way by
saying that proclamation of Jesus as the coming Son of man is the form,
the shape, of his presence in the community. As the one who is coming,
he is present and qualifies the community, which knows it comes from
him, as an eschatological community.

Jesus and Faith

We begin once more with considerations which we employed at the outset of the discussion of the Son-of-man sayings. We proceeded there from the proclamation of Jesus in the presentation by the primitive community. We saw that the one whom the primitive community proclaimed is himself presented as one who proclaims. From the total complex of the proclamation we then lifted out the portion in which a title was the content of the proclamation. We determined that in early tradition the Son of man was still differentiated from Jesus. The apocalyptic concept served to qualify eschatologically the relationship to Jesus and his proclamation.

Now that portion is certainly a very small part of Jesus' proclamation, and we could question whether we have not allowed ourselves to be misled by its peculiar features into formulating specific results too rapidly. We took our starting point in the proclamation and came very quickly to a relationship to *Jesus*. Indeed, we allowed an inexactitude to remain. We conjectured that a development of the tradition underlies Mark 8:38. From "whoever is ashamed of my *words*" there developed "whoever is ashamed of *me* and my words." But we did not then differentiate precisely between the relationship to Jesus and the relationship to his words, since the earlier stage cannot be demonstrated exactly.

Nevertheless, it is precisely here that a considerable problem still exists. If originally it was really only a matter of proclamation, is such proclamation unconditionally bound to Jesus? That is not at first glance the most obvious thing. A proclamation certainly is always carried on by a proclaimer, but its correctness, its credibility, rests nevertheless in itself. It is not bound in that respect to the person of the one who proclaims it.

Thus the question: for what reason did the primitive community not separate the preaching of Jesus from Jesus? It could naturally have as its reason the fact that the primitive community knew about the origin of this proclamation (and certainly it did know about it). This origin was retained. But this way the real question is still not answered. Islam knows about the preaching of Mohammed. He is *the* prophet (just as Islam also sees Jesus as prophet, to be sure as *a* prophet). But despite this elevation of Mohammed, Islam never took the step (to put it by way of comparison) from an implicit to an explicit Christology.

Of course, Islam then also drew a correct conclusion: the Koran was extolled as the norm. The book took the place of the prophet. That was possible because Mohammed, while he was *the* prophet for Islam, was nevertheless (as we would say) *only* a prophet. What was important was his proclamation, not he himself.

When the Christian faith becomes a book-religion, when therefore the book becomes canonical, the same thing has in principle happened here. The book takes the place of Jesus. To put it another way, the book takes the place of the event.

But apparently that was just what the primitive community did not want. It could certainly have announced the nearness of the kingdom, could certainly have attached the call to *metanoia* to it. But it did not do that. Repetition of the *proclamation* of Jesus is thus apparently not the exhaustive expression of what Jesus means for faith.

It is not possible, however, to operate here simply with the concepts of implicit and explicit Christology in the sense that the proclaimer became the one proclaimed. Even though that may later be in the foreground, and even though the explicit qualification of the one proclaimed may support and determine the proclamation (as one can see, for example, in Matthew), it must not be overlooked even at this point that the one proclaimed nevertheless also still continues to proclaim. If we follow back the tradition, an intermediate stage becomes discernible, a transition, which warns us against operating too quickly in terms of a break in the continuity. Mark 8:38 points to this with its opening words: "whoever is ashamed of me and my words. . . ." If we desire to speak here already of an implicit Christology, then we may not say that Jesus' *proclamation* implies a Christology, but rather we must say that *his proclaiming* does so. The relationship remains at this point. We cannot abstract the proclaiming from the one who proclaims, nor can we abstract it from the one who hears either.

Now certainly the question still remains whether the connection to

Jesus is not secondary at this point, to the extent that at first the saying was simply "whoever is ashamed of my *words*. . . ." A second question goes with it, namely, whether it was correct to connect Jesus' proclaiming with Jesus himself, whether it was necessary to do so.

It is clear that, prior to Easter, Jesus' proclaiming could be separated from him only with difficulty, if at all, since in its eschatological urgency it was extraordinary, in that the preaching pointed to the preacher. That certainly occurred without any reflection. From that perspective it is then obvious that the person who heard such proclamation qualified the proclaimer. But would that also have happened if there had been reflection?

Therefore we must now ask whether there are indications that the primitive community qualified Jesus — even apart from his proclaiming — in any special way. We must thus attempt to grasp more clearly whether faith means *Jesus* and not only Jesus' eschatological proclamation. How do we begin to go about that? Let us first mark out the area.

In general it can be said that while we have been dealing thus far with the proclaiming of Jesus, we must now examine his acts. If we take the concept "act" in a general way, we can differentiate between acts that Jesus performs, and those which happen to him. The primitive community reports both kinds. Acts which Jesus performs would then be, for example, healing miracles, nature miracles, raising people from the dead; acts which happen to him would be, for example, the incarnation and the cross.

Acts of the latter type certainly play an important role in Christology, but they are just the ones that do not help us any further in putting our question. The incarnation can only be subsequent to another Christology. Before "becoming flesh" and humiliation can be spoken of, Jesus must be designated as the preexistent one. But that does not happen until a later time. Things are much the same with respect to the cross. It is interpreted only "after the fact." In addition we must give heed to another point: if Jesus *himself* had understood his death on the cross as, for example, an atonement, this would have meant nothing else but that he placed salvation for his followers in the future (something unlikely in view of his assurance of salvation in the present!). Therefore, we must limit ourselves to those acts which Jesus *performed*.

Here also we must make a distinction. There is no doubt that at a later time (and this has happened right down to the present) these acts, these miracles, were understood as a legitimation of Jesus. The argument went thus: because Jesus *could do* that, he was more than a man, and therefore his words are shown to be divine.

This argument is nevertheless unfortunate. The correctness and the credibility of the words depend on the factuality of the miracles. Therefore, credence must be given to the miracles as well. But the concept of faith is shifted if a miracle becomes an article of faith. The classical proof for the impossibility of such argumentation was given by Lessing in his essay "On the Proof of the Spirit and of Power."[48]

Furthermore, what meaning would the refusal by Jesus of the request for a sign then have? If the miracles *confirm* the divinity of Jesus, the refusal of a sign would mean the same as providing an alibi for those who "only" hear. But faith is not supposed to be bound to signs. That does not mean, of course, that signs for their part have nothing to do with faith, but they have to do with faith as signs that are happen*ing*, not as signs that happen*ed*, which then later become articles of faith.

There is still another interpretation of the reported miracles of Jesus. They are not proofs of his divinity, rather they are messianic signs. It was expected that in the last times the blind would see, the lame would walk, the lepers would be cleansed, the deaf would hear, the dead would rise, and the poor would have the gospel preached to them (cf. Matt. 11:5 with Isaiah 35:5 f. and 61:1). That is the answer which Jesus (according to Matthew) gives to the question of John the Baptist. But precisely the juxtaposition of these miracles and signs in chapters 8-10 of the Gospel of Matthew indicates that the miracles were interpreted in this way *at a later time.* Matthew says in this context that in Jesus this messianic time was present. (Luke interprets in a similar way; cf. Luke 7:21 in the context of 7:18-23.)

A christologizing of Jesus thus takes place here by means of the miracles. He is isolated from the relationship, he is set apart as important in himself, he is equipped with a christological predicate and is in that way authorized to command what the disciples are to teach others to observe (Matt. 28:20).

In this way also the point where we must begin can be clearly seen. We can neither isolate the miracles, nor can we isolate Jesus as a miracle worker. We are asking about the primitive community's faith in Jesus.

48. [G. E. Lessing's essay of 1777, with its famous dictum that "accidental truths of history can never become the proof of necessary truths of reason," is conveniently found in English translation in *Lessing's Theological Writings*, ed. Henry Chadwick (Stanford University Press, 1957), pp. 51-56. —EDITOR.]

If we want to investigate this question by means of the acts, we must therefore ask *about the acts in their connection with faith in Jesus*. But we may *not* shift the question in such a way that we *ask about faith in the acts*, and then, *proceeding from that point*, attempt to establish a *connection with Jesus*. It is therefore *not* a matter of christological interpretation of the acts (which was repeatedly done at a later time), *rather* it is a matter of whether connections exist between the acts of Jesus and the christological interpretation of his person.

What we face here is different in principle from what we faced in connection with the proclamation. You can hand yourself over to a proclamation. You can believe it, you can do something "at his word" — even if you do not hear the word until long after the death of the one who proclaimed it. But you cannot give yourself over to a reported miracle. You cannot do something only because of a miracle ("at the word of a miracle"), and therefore you cannot proceed on the basis of faith in a miracle.

There is, admittedly, one exception here: it concerns the people to whom the miracle occurs. But there once again we have, in an authentic way, a relationship. And there is a further exception (to be sure already in a derived sense): it concerns people who were witnesses of the miracle.

The reason for all this lies in the fact that the connection between miracle and faith is bound to the time when the miracle occurred. At some later time the miracle can no longer call a person to faith. At a later time it can only be shown how *at that time* miracle and faith in Jesus were interrelated.

In the light of these considerations, we can now divide the miracles into two groups: (1) implicit christological miracles, that is, those in which the miracle itself brings the relationship of faith to expression in some way; and (2) explicit christological miracles, that is, those which are reported in order to qualify Jesus (for example, messianically), or those which intend to show his power as *theios anēr*. [49]

It is apparent that in our context we need to concern ourselves only with those in the first group — although it must be remarked at the outset that a sure differentiation is not always possible, since the first group has been used later in the sense of the second group (for example, Matthew), and miracles of the second group, even when they are

49. [A Greek phrase meaning "divine man," i.e., one who has divine powers. — TRANSLATOR.]

secondary, are also occasionally presented in the way the miracles in the first group are. For the discussion that follows, I refer to the article by Gerhard Ebeling entitled "Jesus and Faith," to which I owe both the material and much stimulation.[50]

We note first a remarkable statistical finding in the Synoptic Gospels. Apart from the ending to Mark, which is secondary, the term *pisteuein*[51] with its derivatives occurs eighty times, of which sixty-three come from the mouth of Jesus. Of the remaining seventeen occurrences, *pisteuein* is found eleven times in immediate proximity to a saying of Jesus, so that it is fair to conclude that in these instances the sayings of Jesus provide the occasion to speak of faith. The remaining six passages are found in the Lucan infancy narratives (1:20, 45), in the Lucan Easter story (24:11, 41), and once each in the Passion narrative in Mark (15:32) and in Matthew (27:42), that is, in passages where secondary influence is easy to explain. The results, taken as a whole, provide a very interesting parallel to what we found with respect to the concept "Son of man." It can be said that the concept *pisteuein* (with its derivatives) occurs for the most part in the Synoptic material in the direct words of Jesus (or occasioned by them), something which is remarkably similar to the situation with the phrase "Son of man," even though in this case the word does not come quite so exclusively from Jesus himself.

At this point it is possible (in the context of our train of thought) to raise an objection. Do we not remain, with such findings, fundamentally within the framework of Jesus' *proclamation*? That is in the first instance correct, and yet there is a difference here. The concept "Son of man" is found only in *pure* sayings-passages. The concept *pisteuein* appears *also* in pure sayings-passages, but in addition, it occurs in the mouth of Jesus in places where we do not have to do with pure sayings-passages, but rather with passages that belong to narratives, especially to stories about healings. To give only one example at this point, when Jesus says to a man whom he has healed, "Your *pistis*[52] has saved you," that is something quite different from an occasion where he speaks in a theoretical way about faith, or about those of "little faith," or those who have no faith at all, or when he summons to faith.

Thus, the concept of faith leads us even further than the concept of

50. G. Ebeling, "Jesus and Faith," in *Word and Faith,* trans. James W. Leitch (Philadelphia: Fortress, 1963), pp. 201-46.

51. [A Greek verb in the infinitive form meaning "to believe."—TRANSLATOR.]

52. [A Greek word meaning "faith" or "trust."—TRANSLATOR.]

the Son of man, and for that reason now the possibility also exists that our consideration of the concept of faith will lead us further, if we have as our intention a clarification of the connection between *Jesus* and faith, not simply the connection between the proclamation of Jesus and faith. Indeed, it is even the case—Ebeling has called attention to it— that the use of the concept *pisteuein* is relatively uniform in the stories of healing, whereas it is diffuse in the other group.[53]

Of those places where the concept "faith" is used in pure sayings-passages, I want to indicate only one group at this point, a group which stands in very close connection, so far as subject matter is concerned, to the stories about healing, which we must then discuss. This group is constituted around the logion, handed on in various forms, about the power of faith. The oldest form may well be found in Matthew 17:20, "For truly, I say to you, if you have faith as a grain of mustard seed, you will say to this mountain, 'Move hence to yonder place,' and it will move." The contrast in this saying is sharp: the tiny grain of mustard seed, the enormous mountain. Later the comparison with the mustard seed was regarded as inappropriate, because its minuteness gave rise to a misleading interpretation, namely, if you had only a little bit of faith. The variations in the parallel passages are to be explained in this way (Mark 11:23; Matt. 21:21; Luke 17:6). The insignificance of faith, however, is precisely the point. Faith is not visible, but it can do everything.[54]

But what kind of a faith is that? The passage speaks neither of faith in Jesus nor of faith in God. With this question we now come to the stories about healings. They must be seen against the background of this saying, or the other way around, this saying must be seen against the background of the healings-narratives. It cannot be clearly determined what has been influenced by what. In any case, however, it must be said that this saying is without real parallel in the Jewish and late Jewish realms. Concerning its historical authenticity, I should rather not judge. Nevertheless, it is certain that the primitive community has Jesus speak about faith in a way that is without parallel.

Let me enumerate the nine stories of healings which are significant within our context. (1) The paralytic (Mark 2:1-12 par.; Mark 2:5, "When Jesus saw their faith . . ."). (2) The woman with the flow of

---

53. G. Ebeling, "Jesus and Faith" (cited above, n. 50), p. 226.
54. Cf. *ibid.*, pp. 227-29.

blood (Mark 5:25-34 par.; Mark 5:34, *hē pistis sou sesōken se*)[55]
(3) Jairus' daughter (Mark 5:21-24, 35-43 par.; Mark 5:36, "Fear not,
only believe"). (4) The Syrophoenician woman (Mark 7:24-30; Matt.
15:21-28; only Matt. 15:28, "O woman, great is your faith"). (5) Healing of the epileptic child (Mark 9:14-29 par.; Mark 9:23, "All things are
possible to him who believes"; Mark 9:24, "I believe, help my un-
belief"). (6) Healing of Bartimaeus (Mark 10:46-52 par.; Mark 10:52,
hē pistis sou sesōken se).[55] (7) Centurion of Capernaum (Matt. 8:5-13
par.; Matt. 8:10, "Not even in Israel have I found such faith"). (8) Healing of two blind men (Matt. 9:27-31; Matt. 9:28, Jesus asks, "Do you
believe that I am able to do this?"; Matt. 9:29, "According to your faith
be it done to you"). (9) The ten lepers (Luke 17:11-19; Luke 17:19,
hē pistis sou sesōken se).[55] In addition to these nine examples there is a
further negative one, namely, the rejection of Jesus in Nazareth, where
Jesus can perform no mighty act and wonders at their lack of faith
(Mark 6:6). In general, it must also be noted, the parallels display to
some extent certain variations which I have not always given exactly.

The picture is nevertheless clear. *Faith* is always connected here to an
event. The event, in turn, is connected to *Jesus*. Jesus expects faith or
requires faith or attributes the event to faith, especially in the phrase
which occurs seven times in the Synoptics: *hē pistis sou sesōken se*[55]
(Matt. 9:22; Mark 5:34; 10:52; Luke 7:50; 8:48; 17:19; 18:42).

We could, of course, at this point ask again about the historicity of
the events and the words. An answer would be even more difficult than
in the case of Jesus' proclamation. There are special problems in almost
every pericope. The story of the paralytic has apparently been expanded
(Mark 2:5*b*-10 may be secondary); here we encounter, in addition, a
Son-of-man saying from the third group, and the whole pericope is
already far along the way toward an explication of its Christology.[56]
With respect to the stories of the centurion of Capernaum and the
Syrophoenician woman, we probably have to do with variants.[57] The
pericope of the healing of the epileptic child (Mark 9:14) displays at the
very least legendary elements, etc.

Even if there are uncertainties remaining here, however, the point
they have in common is significant, namely, that the primitive commu-

---

55. [A Greek phrase meaning "your faith has saved you." — TRANSLATOR.]
56. Cf. R. Bultmann, *History of the Synoptic Tradition* (cited above, n. 12), pp. 14 f.,
212 f.
57. *Ibid.*, pp. 38 f., 64.

nity represents Jesus' healing in such a way that it stands in connection with faith. Now, with what kind of faith do we have to do here? We said earlier that we wanted to ask about the acts in their connection with faith in Jesus. But it is not a case of faith in Jesus. Rather the concept "faith" is used in an absolute sense. Passages which speak of faith in Jesus (Matt. 18:6) or expressly of faith in God (e.g. Mark 11:22) are not only exceptions, but are consistently more recent from the point of view of tradition history. What kind of a faith is it, then, which is being spoken of in the stories about healing?

We confront here a difficulty similar to the one we faced in relation to the Son-of-man sayings. We determined at that time that the title has been emptied of its content. Only the structure was retained, and it was refilled with new material. This possibility is also to be found in the concept "faith," since in the Old Testament *'mn*[58] is "a general concept the content of which is determined differently in each instance by the particular thing it describes."[59]

Now, to be sure, we cannot immediately determine in our examples to what the faith is directed. But we do find indications. The following parallel is interesting. In Mark 9:23 we read, "Everything is possible to him who believes"; in Mark 10:27, we read, "With God, all things are possible." According to that, the one who believes—believing!—has power, and indeed a power which is the power of God and can do something which, from the point of view of men (without faith), belongs to the *adynata*.[60]

Thus both aspects come into view here. The person who believes is the one who is helpless, who cannot help himself, who has reason (as the stories of the healings clearly show) for despair in the face of the overwhelming power of sickness, whose very existence has been shaken—*and* the one who now (as a believer, in the accomplishment of faith) allows God to act, allows that to happen which only God is able to do.

This faith arises in the encounter with Jesus; it is connected, as the

---

58. [A Hebrew word meaning "faith."—TRANSLATOR.]

59. Arthur Weiser, *"Pisteuō . . . ,"* in *Theologisches Wörterbuch zum Neuen Testament* (Stuttgart: Kohlhammer), 6 (1959), p. 184, lines 19 f.; Eng. trans. in G. Kittel and G. Friedrich, eds., *Theological Dictionary of the New Testament,* trans. G. W. Bromiley (Grand Rapids: Eerdmans), vol. 6 (1968), p. 184: "a formal concept whose content is in each case determined by the specific subj[ect]."; the trans. cited above is that of Dorothea M. Barton, "Bible Key Words," X, *Faith* (London: A. & C. Black, 1961), p. 5.

60. G. Ebeling, "Jesus and Faith" (cited above, n. 50), p. 233. [The Greek word *adynata* means "impossible things" or "things which cannot be done."—TRANSLATOR.]

primitive community expresses it, with the activity of Jesus. It is a faith awakened by Jesus. Its immediacy is revealed itself in the fact that faith is completely undogmatic. It is not oriented to some *concept of God.* No confession of faith was required of the pagans who were healed. Indeed, they apparently did not even know what happened to them. And nevertheless they were told to their face, "It was your faith which saved you." That kind of concrete adjudgment of faith is without prototype.[61]

"If however the faith to which Jesus awakened men was faith as such and by definition faith in God, then it was manifestly a case of concrete faith, i.e., of encountering God concretely."[62] And again we have here a parallel to the sayings about the Son of man. If we spoke there of the *urgent* proximity before which Jesus' proclamation placed a person, then it is a matter, in the call to faith in the activity of Jesus, of the *concrete* proximity of God. Both supplement one another. On the one hand, time is emphasized; on the other hand, it is the reality of the confrontation in the concrete event.

In the context of the sayings about the Son of man, I cited a contribution Bultmann made to the discussion: Jesus disregarded time. We can now modify this sentence. The primitive community presents Jesus' healings in such a way that in them the distance from God is disregarded. Here, also, "disregarding" is to be understood in the sense of a positive qualification, namely, that distance is taken away. There is no distance anymore, because faith is arrived at through Jesus. But faith is power; it is, as Ebeling formulates it, "participation in the omnipotence of God."[63] In the encounter with Jesus, therefore, God is no longer the distant God, but rather the One who is presently active. His nearness occurs in faith. In this sense, Jesus was understood by the primitive community as the initiator of faith.

The stories of healing are therefore basically not stories of healing at all. Rather, they are exemplary stories for the power of faith which is awakened through Jesus. That does not mean that the healing would now be of no consequence; but it does mean that the healing itself is not, and dare not become, the object of faith. What the healing is intended to show is that which faith, that which believing, is able to do — to show what happens where faith is present, and indeed a faith whose initiator is Jesus.

61. *Ibid.,* p. 235; cf. pp. 231 f.
62. *Ibid.,* pp. 235 f.
63. *Ibid.,* p. 241.

With that, however, the stories of healing point to the time prior to Easter. That is not said in the sense of the traditional question about their historicity. None of the stories were written prior to Easter. But they still express the original relationship in such a way that the encounter with the Jesus who acts, leads to faith.

At this point we have to do again with the beginnings of Christology. They are not yet at this point explicit in the later sense. Nevertheless the relationship is a totally christological one, something which is especially clear in that this relationship is again a double one. The first unites the person who is ill with Jesus and awakens faith. The second unites the ill person who has come to faith through Jesus with God. The two of them must be differentiated, even if it is just at this point that no separation is to occur. The relationship to Jesus is the basis of the relationship to God.

But that can, of course, only be expressed from close proximity to the event. The difficulty which arises in later expressions is that an encounter with Jesus that was possible at an earlier time must now also be made understandable as the basis of faith. The difficulty is greater here than in the case of proclamation, since the activity of Jesus is in no way separable from him. How is the problem to be solved?

We can see how in the miracle-stories we listed earlier. The difficulty is bridged in the first instance by making the past, by making Jesus and his activity, the object of proclamation. That does not yet mean that he has also thereby become the object of faith. He is proclaimed as the originator of faith. We must make a precise distinction here. I will return to this once more in my conclusion.

Admittedly, a new problem arises here, namely, how can this statement, which in the last analysis points to the past, be presented as relevant at the present time? The element of time plays a role, together with that of distance. That was also the case with the sayings about the Son of man. The problem there was simpler to solve in that the conception of time was implicitly bound up with the idea of the Son of man. The interim period could be characterized in such a way that the Son of man was declared to be the one who had come and at the same time was expected as the one who was to come.

It is necessary to proceed in a different fashion with the miracles. I referred earlier to Matthew 11:5, "The blind see, the lame walk," etc. Here the *miracles* are interpreted as messianic signs, and in this way the Christology becomes explicit. But it is immediately clear that this is a narrowing-down, since *one* aspect of this far more comprehensive complex of the concrete encounter with the power of God is singled out, namely, the messianic aspect.

It is just at this point that the concept of time enters into this complex. Miracles are expected in the final, messianic time. The time of Jesus is therefore qualified as "messianic time," and Jesus as "the messiah." The result is then that he is believed in as the messiah. But what does that mean? Because Jesus *was* the Messiah, he is therefore legitimated as a new lawgiver. In the redaction of Matthew the miracles, therefore, have the function of qualifying Jesus.

Similarly, it can also happen in the individual story, should such an interest be present, that the uniqueness of the miracle worker (for example, as *theios anēr*) is demonstrated. The process of making the Christology explicit can therefore proceed in a variety of ways.

Before I arrange the various observations which have only been hinted at here and in the preceding section, I should like briefly to discuss a third complex of material.

Jesus and the
Lord's Supper

It is quite clear that I can say only very little about this comprehensive theme, since in the context here, I am concerned primarily with christological problems. I shall, therefore, limit myself to working out the points which are pertinent to our question.

The difficulties involved in getting at the origins of the Lord's Supper are well known. The four reports of the so-called words of institution which have been handed down are all cultic formulations. They inform us concerning the "liturgies" of the Lord's Supper which were in use in the primitive Christian communities. Matthew is obviously dependent on Mark. Luke's alteration of the material at hand is not entirely clear; apparently, influences exerted by the practice of the community play a role here too. The oldest traditions are those of Mark and Paul. We can say of both that, before they were put into their present context, they circulated in isolated form. This can still be clearly seen in the way Paul introduces the tradition in I Corinthians 11:23. A literary-critical analysis of Mark 14 leads to the same conclusion. Now which of these two forms is the older, from the point of view of tradition history? It would appear that a consensus is taking shape at the present time. Along with Günther Bornkamm, W. G. Kummel, Eduard Schweizer, and others, we shall have to decide for Paul. I shall give the two most important arguments, which will also prove to be of significance later on.

First, we must call attention to the Greek phrase *meta to deipnēsai* ("after supper") which appears in the middle of the Pauline formulation and separates the two individual acts, eating and drinking, from one another by stating that a meal lies between them. In Mark, on the contrary, the saying about the wine follows immediately after the saying about the bread. There is agreement now that originally the Lord's Supper was celebrated within the framework of a complete meal. The combination of the two acts occurred only after the meal was omitted.

Thus we can say that on this point the Pauline formulation has preserved a more original trait.

Second, we must call attention to the difference in the second so-
called "word of interpretation." In the Pauline formulation the emphasis falls on the *diathēkē* ("covenant") whereas the Marcan saying
refers to the *haima* ("blood"). If we compare this with the first "word of
interpretation," where both versions relate the bread to the *sōma*
("body"), it becomes apparent that in the form handed on by Paul the
two words are incongruent, while in Mark they are congruent. Even this
observation (at first merely a formal one) suggests that the Marcan setting has harmonized the incongruence in Paul. A simple reason can be
given provisionally for this harmonizing, namely, the omission of the
meal. In that way, one act was made to come immediately after the
other. It then follows, on the basis of stylistic, and especially liturgical,
custom, that parallel sayings should be formulated in parallel fashion.

This reason, however, is not sufficient to determine the question of
priority. It cannot even be the decisive reason. We are faced here only
with a shift in emphasis, from *kainē diathēkē en tō haimati Iēsou* ("new
covenant in the blood of Jesus") in Paul to *haima tēs diathēkēs* ("blood
of the covenant") in Mark, but also a shift in content, which, in turn,
then made the meal superfluous. We must now investigate that.

If, as the phrase *meta to deipnēsai* indicates, the Lord's Supper was
originally celebrated within the framework of a meal, the two acts of the
Lord's Supper did not occur one after the other, but were rather separated from each other by a short period of time. That meant, in the first
place, that both had to be intelligible in themselves. Interpretation in
this earlier form therefore did not proceed from the parallelism; rather,
it sought to interpret the individual acts independently of each other.
But that means, in the second place (and this has been virtually ignored
until now in all discussion of this problem), that we must ask about the
connection of the individual acts to the meal. They were embedded in
that meal. Can we then, working back from the later development, act
as though we have to do here with two isolated acts, the *only* acts that
had meaning in the framework of the entire meal? Ought we not to
proceed precisely from the unity of the meal? In the light of this observation the Pauline saying about the cup is instructive. When the cup,
which was passed around to the whole community, is designated as
kainē diathēkē, it is immediately clear that it is not an "element" (wine)
which is being interpreted here, but rather the cup which is passed

around, in which all participants at the meal share. In sharing in the cup, the community shared in the *kainē diathēkē*. Indeed, it *is* this *kainē diathēkē* — as the added interpretation shows, by virtue of, or by reason of, the blood of Christ, which means by virtue of his death, here understood as an atoning death. The saying about the cup therefore has an ecclesiological character, the ecclesiological reference being grounded in the christological (*haima*).

The saying about the bread, on the other hand, is primarily christological in orientation. Here the basic idea is that of sacramental *communio*. Those who eat of the bread are granted participation in the *sōma Christou*. Here one must not ask whether it is the glorified body (the *doxa*-body) of the exalted one, or the body of Jesus which was given in death that is intended. The two are identical. Participation in the *sōma Christou* must be understood in an entirely realistic sense. To be sure, this christological factor contains implicitly once more an ecclesiological factor. Whether that is already the case in Paul's *formula* cannot be determined from the formula itself. *Paul*, however, interprets it in that way when he says in I Corinthians 10:17, "Because there is *one* loaf, we who are many are *one* body, for we all partake of the same loaf."

If we now turn from Paul to Mark, the displacement that has occurred is clearly seen. The second saying points no longer to the *diathēkē*, but rather to the *haima*. The cup which circulates through the congregation is no longer meant, but rather the contents of the cup, the wine. The body and blood of Christ are now understood as the two constituents of the Christ who was given into death. The sacramental realism is attached to the elements. The first element is identified with the body, the second with the blood of Christ. This step was destined to have decisive significance for the later development of the Supper. At first, however, this was by no means the case. If it had been the intention to interpret the elements in a parallel way, the concept *sōma* would hardly have been chosen. Rather, it would have to have been *sarx*, since *sarx kai haima* ("flesh and blood") constitute the "whole man."

We can, therefore, perceive in the movement from Paul to Mark a displacement from a celebration within the framework of a meal — in which at least the saying about the cup still indicates the connection to the communal meal — to an orientation focusing on the elements.

Keeping that in mind, let us seek now to penetrate behind the tradition in Paul. Whence does it come? Paul relates it to the night in which the *kyrios*, the Lord, was handed over. Mark (or a redactor before him) proceeds in a similar way when he places the cultic formula into an older account of the Passion, and thus turns the formula for the first time into "words of institution."

Now, this etiology is *theologically* understandable. The question is whether it is also tenable *historically*. There are objections to the latter. To begin with, it is peculiar that there should have been an account of the Passion without any words of institution. If the Lord's Supper was instituted in the night of the betrayal, then it was also celebrated, and it could hardly be passed over in the composition of an account of the Passion. If, on the other hand, a Lord's Supper was celebrated whose point of origin had not yet been traced back to that night, then it could not be mentioned there.

Further objections arise out of our earlier considerations of the primitive community's proclamation of the eschatology of Jesus. The institution of a cult presupposes that a church had been planned for the time beyond Jesus' death and, therefore, for the future. That that was the case prior to Easter is improbable (at least according to the Son-of-man sayings). It must be pointed out further that the sacramental *communio* is hardly to be derived from Jewish conceptions, but that the decisive interpretative factors in the accounts of the Lord's Supper presuppose Jesus' death as a saving event, an interpretation which surely did not arise until the post-Easter period. As a result it will have to be said that we can hardly speak of the *institution* of the Lord's Supper as an act which occurred in the night of the betrayal and which was meant to be repeated as a cultic activity.

Is Bultmann, therefore, correct when (following Heitmüller, and others) he designates the account of the Lord's Supper as an "etiological cultic legend"? We shall have to answer in the affirmative if we assume that the celebration of the Lord's Supper *originated* somewhere else (in the Hellenistic Christian community, it may then be presumed), and that its point of origin was then placed back into the time of Jesus. But are these presuppositions valid? Before we answer that question, we must attempt to work our way to Paul's tradition concerning the Lord's Supper from the other direction, i.e., from backgrounds in Judaism and Jesus' activities. To do so we must enter an area which is not particularly clear from the point of view of tradition history. We do find hints there, however, which can give us indications about the early development.

Reference has frequently been made to the fact that the accounts of the feeding miracles in the Gospels contain terminology which appears in the accounts of the Lord's Supper—to be more exact, we would have to say terminology which *also* appears in the accounts of the Lord's Supper. The common root is the Jewish meal. But this meal also plays a further role in the Gospels. We hear repeatedly of fellowship meals with Jesus—those which especially must be mentioned are the meals where the table-companions are tax collectors and sinners, men, therefore, who were cultically unclean. If we remember, on the one hand, that every Jewish meal (simply by reason of the prayer spoken at it) is a cultic meal, and, on the other hand, that the consummation is often represented with the picture of a meal or is conceived as a communal meal, then the eschatological character which the early community saw in these meals of Jesus becomes clear.

Once again we encounter here the double relationship: in their relationship to Jesus, a relationship established in the table fellowship, sinners and tax collectors stand at the same time in the eschatological relationship. In this sense we can say with Fuchs that Jesus' *activity* implies a Christology.[64] In eating and drinking with Jesus, the primitive church experiences a fellowship which it declares to be eschatological.

After Easter the church continued to celebrate this meal (according to Acts 2:42–47, with *agalliasis*, "exultation") and indeed as the church which now understood itself as the eschatological community, as the community of the *kainē diathēkē*. They celebrated this meal in their houses, and they did it as a complete meal. That they did so is not only quite understandable, it was in fact the natural thing to do. The common meal was the expression of closest communion and intimate fellowship. Christian worship did not yet exist, but there were eschatological communities which assembled for a meal and in that way carried on the tradition of the meals with Jesus.

Soon the community put into words, it formulated, that which it experienced in these meals and the way it understood them. The content of these meals became explicit. We now have before us something corresponding to what has already confronted us on other occasions in the transition from an implicit to an explicit Christology.

The interpretation of the meal then made use of concepts which were available in Judaism and in the Hellenistic mystery cults. Therefore we cannot say that the Lord's Supper is to be derived from the religious

---

64. Ernst Fuchs, "Glaube und Geschichte," in *Zeitschrift für Theologie und Kirche*, 53 (1957), 130, *et passim*.

environment of primitive Christianity, but it is true that the means of interpreting the Lord's Supper were taken from there. These two points must be kept clearly distinct from one another. In carrying out exegesis on the Lord's Supper, one will, of course, ask about the origin of the concepts which are employed, but in principle it makes no difference, provided those concepts are able, to some extent, at least, to express the content of the meal. It is indeed only "to some extent," since here too the explication can never adequately express the complete content.

The interpretative material used in relation to the bread and the cup was attached to prayers at the beginning and at the conclusion of the meal. The breaking of the bread at the beginning and the handing around of the cup at the end are thus accentuated, but they are not separated from the meal as a whole and turned into the main thing. At first nothing more is affected than the points within the total meal at which the meal itself is interpreted. We have to do here with quasi-liturgical portions of the meal which simply offered themselves to be used in working out the meaning. The fact that precisely *here,* however, interpretations could be attached was bound to be of great consequence for the entire further development of the Lord's Supper.

It is my opinion that this process of making the meal explicit in meaning through interpreting certain of its features did not take place in a purely Jewish-Christian, but rather in a Hellenistic-Jewish-Christian, environment (insofar as the development is today still visible at all). For its interpretation of the bread as *sōma* the celebrating community took over analogies from the mystery cults. The motif of the *kainē diathēkē* originates in Jewish concepts.

Thus we are saying that two features are connected in the meal: expression of the new eschatological community, and in it the presence of Jesus. Both are then grounded in the cross. The *sōma* is the *sōma hyper hymōn* ("body which is for you"); the *diathēkē* is the *diathēkē en tō haimati Iēsou* ("covenant in the blood of Jesus"). Later (we have already seen this in the transition to the formulation in Mark) the point of emphasis shifts. The presence of the *kyrios* is now bound to the food, to the "elements."

But with this step the meal, which originally occupied the central position as the meal of the *kainē diathēkē,* has been robbed of its meaning. It is eliminated. Only the two fixed points which have been accentuated by the interpretation remain. They now come one after the other. Hence the interpretations are adjusted to one another. In the saying about the cup the *haima* is emphasized in place of the *diathēkē*. *Sōma* and *haima* are then understood as *sarx kai haima,* as body *and* blood, as the two parts of the body of Jesus.

A sacramental stage (in the narrower sense) is thereby reached. The fellowship character of the meal is almost completely lost. In any case this communal character is (due to the fact that the meal has disappeared) no longer immediately apparent and is no longer constitutive. The food becomes (according to Ignatius' *Epistle to the Ephesians* 20:2) *pharmakon athanasias* [a "medicine of immortality"], an antidote against dying. The food contains the powers of the world beyond. The eschatological community has become a cultic community. The food is received at the altar, but it can also be taken (as holy food) to the sick who could not attend the church service.

I have already remarked that explicit Christology is, in principle, less important than so-called implicit Christology. That seems to me to be particularly evident in the case of the Lord's Supper. The fact that "less" emerges at the explicit stage came about ordinarily because an earlier, complex understanding was channeled in one specific direction and thereby narrowed in scope, through the way in which concepts which had been formulated earlier (for example, Son of man, Messiah, Son of God) were employed as interpretative material. If these concepts are allowed to stand, and if they are then amplified by means of others, the result is a variety of Christologies which dare not be combined or harmonized, but which, again and again, as explications, point backward, precisely to the original, more complex conception.

In the case of the Lord's Supper, however, the matter is somewhat different. Here *one* explication has received further development. But in this instance every new stage of development represents a further departure from the previous one. As a result, only a torso has remained, namely, the real presence of the *kyrios* in the holy food. In that way *one* decisive impulse has, to be sure, been retained; even at the outset, there was something on the order of "real presence" — only it was not bound to a specific place, to a specific element. What has been lost is the impulse of eschatological existence, which is what came to expression precisely in the fellowship of members at the common meal. The table of the Lord is no longer the table about which the members sit, as *kaine͞ diathēkē*; rather it is the table *before* which the member sits and which he approaches.

In conclusion, we take up once more the question whether the accounts of the institution are to be designated as "etiological cultic legends." In the form in which we have them, they have already evoked a process of historicization.[65] Liturgy has been "given a date," its point of origin is named. That is, of course, unhistorical. To that extent, we can in fact speak of etiological cultic legends, because the Lord's Supper, in the form which it has now attained and in which it is now celebrated, is referred back to the words of institution.

And yet this characterization of the Supper as "etiological cult legends" remains an unhappy one, because the celebration itself is older than its liturgy. Certainly the liturgy does not go back to Jesus. But the Lord's Supper itself has its point of origin in the fellowship meals with Jesus prior to Easter, meals which his followers understood as placing them in the eschatological relationship.

65. E. Fuchs, *Das Urchristliche Sakramentverständnis* (Bad Cannstatt: R. Müllerschön, 1958), pp. 16 f.

Christological Perspectives

The material which can be offered in such a brief presentation as this naturally represents much too meager a foundation for one to be able to erect upon it the edifice of a history of Christology. I shall, therefore, not try to do that at this point. But I should like, nevertheless, to pick up certain observations and results from our study, and I should like to draw out some of the lines which will help in ordering and arranging the whole.

Let us begin that task once more with form criticism, because it represents something like the pivotal point of the christological problem. Form criticism had led to the insight that the material which has been handed on has been shaped not by historical, but rather by kerygmatic, interests. It was therefore faith which shaped the tradition. That occurred in the period following Easter. It occurred in the community, on the basis of one or several situations within the life of the community (*Sitze im Leben*). I am of the opinion that all of these conclusions are correct. Nevertheless, it behooves us to exercise caution at this point, because the danger exists that the individual elements of these form-critical results will be combined with one another too quickly and therefore in an inappropriate manner. Bornkamm, for example, formulates the matter in the following way: from the very beginning of the post-Easter history, "the preacher Jesus of Nazareth enters into the message of faith and himself becomes the content of the preaching: he who called men to believe is now believed in."[66]

But can that really be said in that way? I think modification is necessary because a whole series of stages in the development have been passed over in that sentence. It is certainly correct to say that the one who called men to believe, *later* becomes the one believed in. It is even

66. *Jesus of Nazareth* (cited above, n. 17), p. 179.

possible to speak of discontinuity in a certain sense, if beginning and
end are put side by side. But is it possible to begin this explicit Christology so early? Was it already active at the beginning of the history
following Easter? If that were the case, it would be very difficult to
explain how it happens that traditions have been handed on which
show no awareness at all of this discontinuity (namely, that the one
who calls men to believe becomes the one believed in).

Nevertheless, let us proceed step by step. The proclaimer becomes the
one proclaimed. That is correct, because it can hardly be disputed that
the historical Jesus was a proclaimer. But the fact that he became the
one proclaimed is not connected with Easter, nor ought we to unite it
immediately with the fact that the one proclaimed was now also the one
believed in. In the first instance, Jesus is the one proclaimed to the extent that the proclamation has him as its content. But he is also the
content of the proclamation when he is himself still represented as one
who proclaimed.

The frequently repeated formulation that Jesus became the one proclaimed may in no wise overlook the question concerning *who* he was
proclaimed as being: as one who in his preaching ignores time, as one
who in his acts ignores the distance to God, as one who in the fellowship
of the meal gives eschatological fellowship—or as one who is believed in.
None of these are identical. We are not allowed to bring Pauline
theology into play so quickly in connection with our reflections which
center around the complex of Easter. We will have to say more about
that in a moment. In any case, the findings from the Synoptic material
show us that Jesus was not so quickly proclaimed as the one believed in.
Nevertheless, he is from the beginning the one who is proclaimed.

But what part, then, does Easter play here? That cannot be determined so clearly. We may certainly assume that not a line in the
Synoptic material (as we have it today) was *written down* before Easter,
but we have nevertheless seen that some traditions very probably reach
back into the period prior to Easter. The early statements of the community are oriented toward the immediate encounter with Jesus. But
precisely there, it is worth noting, an *ascertainable* influence exercised
by Easter on the formation of the tradition does not exist, or is quite
minimal.

But what, then, is the status of the judgments made by form criticism? Is it still possible to say that the tradition has been shaped by

faith? If faith is immediately understood to mean "Easter faith," then it is naturally problematic. We must therefore ask what kind of faith it was which influenced the formation of the tradition. It was not faith *in* Jesus, as it seems to me the material quite clearly indicates, but rather it was the faith awakened by Jesus. Men who have come to faith through Jesus, and that means, those who have been placed in the eschatological relationship, proclaim what part Jesus, in his words and his deeds, had in that event. That *could* clearly have happened before Easter. Even if we do not have a single actual illustration of that, it is hardly conceivable that it did not happen. The activity of Jesus did not take place in the exclusivity of a small circle. The reports about him circulated everywhere (Mark 1:28). There must have existed both neutral historical reports about him and testimony growing out of personal involvement. In this testimony, Jesus was already always the one who was proclaimed. Such testifying proclamation then also occurred after Easter; but in that, Easter itself plays no role, at least not directly.

That, of course, does not mean that Easter can simply be ignored. An indirect influence certainly does exist, because the basis for the later continuation of this preaching, despite the death of Jesus on the cross, is surely to be found in Easter. We can, therefore, say that Easter represents the *presupposition* for further proclamation of Jesus. The fact, the *"that,"* of the proclamation goes back to Easter. The *formation,* on the other hand, goes back to the faith which was awakened by Jesus, a faith which nonetheless did not shatter on the cross, because of Easter.

We have now traced several traditions backward and in part also forward. What appears to me to be noteworthy is the fact that there can be no talk of rigid boundaries, of a break, occasioned by Easter. I would certainly resist the conclusion if it were to be drawn from this that there is a line of continuity which begins with the historical Jesus, possibly with his self-consciousness, and then carries over without a break into the community. We cannot avoid the establishment and acceptance of the oft-mentioned break which form criticism has opened up. Only we have to define it somewhat more exactly than is usually the case.

Let us consider here what is normally understood by this break. It marks the boundary between the historical Jesus and the community. To put it another way, it separates Jesus' preaching and the preaching of the community about him. It must be conceded that this break becomes visible only after Easter. But in the last analysis that is connected

simply with the fact that we do not have any material from the time
prior to Easter. This break, however, does not have its basis in Easter
itself. It is connected much more with faith, which again, however,
cannot simply be identified with Easter faith. The break lies at the point
where a believer proclaims Jesus' words and deeds. But that happened
already before Easter. Let me amplify that briefly.

We must take into account the point that we can in no way reach the
historical reality which lies on the other side of the break, and that it is
from that reality alone that we could confirm the existence of the break.
In all existing material Jesus is always the content of a *proclamation*.
We also lack any line from a neutral, historical observer. We are, therefore, not able to represent in chronological sequence "historical Jesus —
proclamation," and then determine that a break lies between them.

We can only proceed in the opposite way, that is, we can only raise
our questions moving backwards from the proclamation. Since it is
believers who proclaim what significance Jesus has for their faith, the
break between this proclamation and the historical Jesus lies in the fact
of the proclamation itself that grows out of faith. The break is already
present in the moment that a statement about Jesus is made from the
perspective of one pole of the relationship "Jesus — believer" (as I said in
my introduction). We could now ask whether, in that case, we ought to
speak about a break anymore at all. If we do speak of it, we must indicate that it is a methodological break, a break which is made necessary
by the method of asking the question. This break is, of course, not to be
overplayed, since it marks the limit of the possibility of *historical* questioning. The last dimension which can be reached remains the statement of a believer, not that of a historical observer. In our material it is
always the case that a believer makes a statement about Jesus.

In *this* sense the beginnings of Christology certainly lie in the community. But it is clear that something else entirely is meant by that, than
when Christology is otherwise said to arise in the community. But then
it is also clear that there no longer exists a break in principle between
implicit and explicit Christology. When I say that, I do not have the
intention, for example, of nullifying or arguing away the very considerable christological differences which lie between the initial and a later
stage of the development. Certainly the content of the preaching
appears different at a later time than it does at the beginning, but this
difference cannot be expressed by saying that the proclaimer becomes

the one proclaimed. Rather, the continuity, which reaches all the way back into the time prior to Easter, exists in the fact that Jesus is always the one who is proclaimed—even when he himself appears as the proclaimer.

To be sure, the picture of the one proclaimed is then also altered. How does that occur? I have given several examples of that. In summary, it could perhaps be expressed in this way: the *function* of Jesus, namely, to call men to faith, to bring men into the eschatological relationship, is expressed, more and more, as time goes on, by qualifying or interpreting his *person.* The range of variations is quite large. He is represented as a man with special power, as a divine miracle-worker, as one who understands mysteries, etc. Or titles are transferred to him: Son of man, Son of God, Christ. We saw a special form in the tradition of the Lord's Supper, where the christological-ecclesiological function of the meal becomes objectified in the elements.

It is necessary, it seems to me, to be very careful in the evaluating of this whole development. Even at this point it is not yet the case that the one proclaimed becomes the one believed in, or that the concept of faith must be modified. There is a difference whether faith has as its object Jesus *as* messiah, or whether it is faith *in* Jesus *the* Messiah. If faith has as its object Jesus *as* Messiah, or *as* Son of man, the functional impulse still lies implicitly in this explicitly christological statement. The functional impulse has only been solidified, and I have already indicated that this terminological solidification can always express only one aspect of the function of Jesus. It therefore says less and is also to be used only in a limited way, namely, only in that situation where the conceptions from which the title is taken, are known and are familiar. If the titles move into another area, they quickly lose their content, as for example, the title "Christ" shows.

In all of this, the transition has now been prepared so that the one proclaimed also becomes, in the full sense, the one believed in. That happens with varying degrees of rapidity, and the concepts often become confused. It must be noted here that the concept of faith in the New Testament is not uniform.

Paul, for example, can speak in a thoroughly functional-christological way. He can say that with Christ *pistis* ("faith") has come (Gal. 3: 23-25), a faith which replaces the "old man"—*nomos* ("law") relationship with that of *huiothesia* ("sonship"). He can say that the new creation which has come into being came because God reconciled the world to himself in Christ (II Cor. 5:17 ff.). On the other side, however, Paul can speak of the *kyrios* almost in the sense of a cultic deity. Precisely the terminology which originates in Hellenistic representations presses most strongly to give expression to Jesus as the one believed in—just as it was quite probably Hellenistic influences which started and hastened the objectification of the functional impulse in the Lord's Supper.

Yet nevertheless, Paul does not lose the connection to history. Faith (*pistis*) comes from hearing (*akoē*) (Rom. 10:17); preaching has as its content the crucified one (I Cor. 2:2), in whom God prepared salvation. Thus we also have in Paul basically two relationships. The one is established through the proclamation, through the *euangelion* ("Gospel"). The other, Paul expresses by the word *huiothesia,* most often by the word *dikaiosynē* ("righteousness," "justification"). But just as it is necessary to differentiate *even* in Paul, it is also necessary at this point not to separate.

Our difficulties in understanding are due in part to the fact that we use the idea of faith differently than Paul does. To be sure, usage is not uniform with him, as it is not with us. Basically for him, however, *pistis* is the acceptance of the kerygma.[67] This kerygma has Christ as its content, and thus Paul can often speak of *pistis eis Christon* ("faith in Christ") and similar phrases, but this formulation is basically an abbreviation for the way of salvation made accessible in Christ.

Let us compare that with the concept of faith as it meets us in the Synoptic tradition. There it expresses the relationship of man to God which is established by the encounter with Jesus. In Paul, the relationship of man to God is designated as *dikaiosynē*, etc., which is established by *pistis* (which equals acceptance of the kerygma). Whoever accepts the message about the salvation which has been prepared by the coming of Christ believes, and he is justified before *God* as a believer. Or to put it another way: he stands in a right relationship to God. Therefore, the Synoptic encounter with Jesus corresponds to Pauline *pistis*; Synoptic *pistis* corresponds to Pauline *dikaiosynē*.

It is possible to follow this line of development still further. I have

<hr>

67. R. Bultmann, "*Pisteuō . . .,*" in *Theologisches Wörterbuch* (cited above, n. 59), 6 (1959), p. 218, line 21, and p. 209, n. 258. Eng. trans. in *Theological Dictionary of the New Testament* (cited above, n. 59), 6, p. 217 and p. 208 n. 258; in *Faith* (cited above, n. 59), p. 87 and p. 69, n. 2.

previously set forth the thesis in another place[68] that the redaction of the Gospel of Mark represents an attachment of Pauline elements to those of the Synoptic tradition. With these questions, however, we would be led far beyond the problems of christological beginnings. Let me simply indicate once more the general tendency. It moves in the direction of combining the two relationships of which I have repeatedly spoken. Where they come together, there the one who initiates, who is the basis for, who originates, who arouses, faith — at this point truly, in the fullest sense, the one in whom faith is to be placed — becomes then also the one who is believed in.

In conclusion, let us ask this question: if the picture which I have sketched out is correct in essentials, what are the consequences to be drawn from it? Christology is not only a problem in the New Testament, it is also a problem for systematic theology. And it is not superfluous to be reminded that it was theological questions *also,* yes, perhaps first and foremost, theological questions, which have set in motion the "problem of Jesus" anew for scholarship. To put it crudely, the problem had ended with Bultmann. Only the post-Easter kerygma had theological significance. Therefore, not only do we not need to go back to Jesus, we are not even to desire to — for that would represent the desire for a security which does not accord with the subject, indeed, a security which is basically predicated on a lack of faith. The point that was then raised concerned "kerygma-theological Docetism," the danger of which was seen to arise here. The *"extra nos"* [Christ "beyond us"] was lacking, etc. Therefore, the demand that Jesus not be renounced was raised *also* for theological reasons.

Since Ernst Käsemann's article, several works have appeared which in fact go further back in the tradition than Bultmann thought was correct or necessary. Scholars began once more to speak of Jesus' proclamation, and attempted to get behind the oldest strata of tradition in a historical way.

I have been in this respect, I am convinced, more careful than some scholars are at the present time. I have developed the methodological

---

68. Willi Marxsen, *Der Evangelist Markus: Studien zur Redaktionsgeschichte des Evangeliums* (Göttingen: Vandenhoeck und Ruprecht, 1959), pp. 91 f., 145 f.; Eng. trans. *Mark the Evangelist: Studies on the Redaction History of the Gospel,* trans. Roy A. Harrisville et al. (Nashville: Abingdon, 1969), pp. 136–38, 213–16.

reasons which restrain me from jumping over in a historical way the relationship between Jesus and the believer. We have, therefore, attained no greater knowledge about the historical Jesus — and yet we have nevertheless passed beyond the break which is supposed to have its locus at Easter.

Thus the history of proclamation is presented to us as a history of Christology which begins as close to Jesus as possible, and as close as our traditions permit us a glimpse. This christological proclamation begins (from a purely temporal point of view) long before the New Testament, runs throughout the New Testament, and passes on into the theological formulations of the early church. There is a break therefore between a so-called implicit and explicit Christology only to the extent that it is a matter of a *conceptual* explication. The transitions are, however, by no means sharp. They take place gradually, and not in a uniform fashion in all localities. What we have in the New Testament, what exegesis of the New Testament can lift out, is a section of this development from the years between about A.D. 50 to 130.

Systematic theology, however, calls attention to the fact that the main point is *Jesus*. In that case, *New Testament* exegesis can help only in an indirect way. There must be exegesis of the sources, after the sources have been revealed by literary criticism. The important matter for systematic theology therefore is to make this whole, often intricate, work on the sources fruitful theologically. If the important point really is Jesus, then the theological problem of Christology cannot be solved simply by showing that the statement accords with Scripture. It is precisely the *direct* orientation to the New Testament which does not yield advancement, since such an orientation comes into contact only with *later* proclamation. This orientation to the New Testament can lead to Docetism in just the same way as retreat to the kerygma can. The problem of how we can avoid a "kerygma-theological Docetism" corresponds precisely to the other problem of how we can avoid a canon-theological Docetism.

It is my opinion that at this point we face considerable problems and tasks. I shall put only three questions which are connected with our problems. What is to be said, in face of the findings concerning the Son-of-man sayings, to theological statements about the return of Christ? What is to be said, in face of the problem of Jesus and faith, to the idea that Jesus is the *object* of faith? And, what is to be said, in face of the early history of the Lord's Supper, to the tiresome controversy over the "elements"? Completely new themes would be involved in answering these questions. But one thing can surely be said, namely, that the task is today a good deal more difficult than it once was.

And yet, when we have learned to understand the New Testament as a portion of the history of proclamation, it will lead us to ask about the "text" of this proclamation. Then it will guide us on the way back, guide us to this "text," to the one who initiates faith—to the one whom the disciples at that time experienced as the one who brought them to faith by his word, by his deeds, and by his fellowship; the one who in manifold ways for almost two thousand years has time and again brought men to faith; to the one who, in our world also, desires, as the one proclaimed, to be the one who initiates faith.

PART TWO

The Lord's Supper

as a

Christological Problem

Prologue

The title, "The Lord's Supper as a Christological Problem," is intentionally so worded and contains implicitly a thesis. Let me summarize that thesis here and sketch the course for our considerations.

In Christology one can show development from an "implicit" to an "explicit" Christology, from a Christology that is indirect to one that is direct, from a "Christology in action" to a considered Christology. Exactly the same development can be shown when one traces the early history of the Lord's Supper. Such is our thesis.

This will be the procedure: in the first section, I shall sketch out very briefly the development of early Christology; in the second part—and parallel to the first—the early development of the Lord's Supper; in a third section, I shall inquire, finally, into the theological consequences which result from our findings.

The Development of
Christology in the
Early Church

The early Synoptic tradition (*Traditionsgut*) shows that Jesus did not call for faith in himself, nor did he apply any of the traditional titles to himself ("Christ," "Son of man," "Son of God"). Later, certainly, both things were done by the church; these (and other) titles were applied to him, and the community's faith was oriented on him.

Easter is usually designated as the turning point. Admittedly, this is too imprecise. The Sayings source, Q, shows us that after Easter the Jesus-tradition was taken up and further proclaimed. At this state there is—at least at first—still no noticeable change in the content of the proclamation. Neither the cross nor Easter itself gets to be included in the content of the proclamation. That point might appear most remarkable. The very fact that the Jesus-tradition is further proclaimed is an indication of something: the congregation knows that what Jesus had brought did not come to a halt with his crucifixion, with his death, that Easter had rather put it in motion again. This fact, the "that" (*"Dass"*) of this post-Easter preaching, the "that" of further proclamation of the Jesus-tradition after Good Friday, has its basis in Easter. Easter is not unfolded in terms of content, but it appears in the "that" of the proclamation. To put this in another way: the Jesus-tradition (especially that in the Sayings source) never says what Easter is—in terms of content; but *that* there is this tradition (as a further proclamation of the Jesus-tradition) has its basis in Easter.

What is the Jesus-tradition all about? We can formulate it very briefly: by his words and deeds Jesus puts men before God.

Here are some examples. The Son of man who is expected at the end of time will judge on the basis of how men react now to Jesus. This means, Jesus anticipates the future. *Now already* (and, indeed, in men's reaction toward him and to his call) occurs the final decision (the one that is valid at the end, the eschatological decision). —Jesus calls men (yes, even publicans and sinners) to his table, into his fellowship. Thus he anticipates the table fellowship of the last times in the kingdom of God. *Now already* men may participate in it. —Jesus brings men to faith. This is frequently made explicit in the stories about healing miracles. That is, men, as believers (as those who have been brought to faith by Jesus), allow to happen to them what God alone can do. "Your faith has saved you." When Jesus speaks to men, he awakens faith in them; he thereby makes them into men who are grounded in God.

One could multiply examples. What is characteristic always is that we are faced with an *action*. Though Jesus is not given any qualifying titles, though he himself does not appear as the "object of faith," he it is who in word and deed makes God actual for men.

At this point we cannot as yet speak of a Christology, at least not in the sense that the *person* of Jesus of Nazareth is interpreted christologically. Nevertheless, what happens here is attached to *Jesus* —and exclusively to him. If, then, what happens here is the actualizing of God through Jesus, one might therefore call what has come to expression *Christology in action*. What is essential in this is the emphasis on function; what happens is always attached to Jesus. That it can be done by him alone is, however, expressed by describing his function, "in action," as it were, and not yet by entitling his person.

We can formulate all this very pointedly by saying that what matters is not Jesus, his quality, his being, or his place in relation to God, but his function, but with this further emphatic qualification: it is *his* function. The assertions about the action appear in various forms in the Jesus-tradition; the functions as such differ greatly. Common to all of them, however, is their eschatological character; the functions are those by which the eschaton is actualized.

After Easter the Jesus-tradition was further proclaimed. The implication is that what Jesus brought is after Easter brought further, but without his physical presence. The danger thereby arises that proclamation will become doctrine. If so, the message would no longer be "*Jesus* makes God actual," "*Jesus* anticipates the future," "On *Jesus* depends the final decision"; but instead, "*There is the possibility* to experience now already the actualizing of God, already now to anticipate the future." If Jesus is placed in brackets, the kerygma would become a doctrine or an ideology. This danger arises precisely because Jesus is no longer visibly present. In that case, he would, to be sure, be the person

who in the past had started the whole business, but he would nonetheless be superfluous for the present.

So it is that now—in order not to lose Jesus—there begins what is
properly a christologizing process. All this is expressed not by saying
that it originated with someone who happened to be Jesus of Nazareth,
but that this eschatological event was possible and also remains possible
only because Jesus was the eschatological messenger.

The action now becomes the object of reflection; and it is reflected
upon, first and foremost, in terms of "person." To use the language
employed above, one might say here too that the "that" of the further
proclamation of the Jesus-tradition is made explicit.

Because this happens after Easter and in light of Easter, vastly differing Christologies can now exist side by side. Their intention is not,
indeed, to describe Jesus of Nazareth historically, but to underscore the
eschatological action as *eschatological* action, giving eschatological
accreditation to the messenger. "Christology in action" becomes now a
considered Christology (the indirect Christology becomes direct, the
implicit becomes explicit). We can trace this development very clearly
in the Synoptics. Paul, who himself presents practically no Jesus-
tradition at all, reflects Christology in an especially intensive way but
stays oriented to the "that" of the humanity of Jesus.

For our purposes this must suffice. Out of our brief sketch two points
are established. At the outset stands the assertion of an action, a function. Out of this comes an assertion about him from whom action and
function derive. His "person" is interpreted, as people give expression to
the emphases of function and action while reflecting upon the person.

It is now my contention that a development analogous to this unfolding of Christology is to be found also in the tradition about the Lord's
Supper.

The Development
of the Lord's Supper
in the Early Church

The place to begin is with several problems on which there is a consensus in scholarship today. The four so-called accounts of the institution of the Lord's Supper (*Einsetzungsberichte*) may be described as "cult-formulas" or as communion "liturgies," even if here and there they have been given a literary reworking. The *Sitz im Leben* in any case is cultic. This means that we learn from these formulas how and with what understanding people celebrated the Lord's Supper at the time these formulas were written down. In this way, then, even the not inconsiderable differences among them are to be explained, even though, as noted, not only further liturgical development, but also literary recasting through a changed understanding of the Lord's Supper may have been at work here.

As to the history of the tradition, it can be safely said that the form in which Matthew has the account is a further development of that given by Mark. The Lucan form (which raises many problems precisely because of its different textual variants) might well be a mixture containing features derived from the Marcan as well as the Pauline accounts.

We must therefore begin with a comparison of the last two formulas mentioned. It is immediately noticeable that both the Marcan and the Pauline accounts are easily detached from their contexts, an indication that at an earlier stage they had once circulated independently. Let us cite the two formulas side by side.

Mark 14:22–24: And as they were eating, he took bread, and blessed, and broke it, and gave it to them, and said, "Take; this is my body [*sōma*]." And he took a cup, and when he had given thanks he gave it to them, and they drank of it. And he said to them, "This is my blood of the covenant [*haima tēs diathēkēs*], which is poured out for many." (RSV)

I Corinthians 11:23–25: For I received [as tradition] from the Lord what I also delivered to you, that the Lord Jesus on the night when he was betrayed took bread, and when he had given thanks, he broke it, and said, "This is my body [*sōma*] which is for you. Do this in remembrance [*anamnēsis*] of me." In the same way also [supply, "he took"] the cup, after supper [*meta to deipnēsai*], saying. "This cup is the new covenant [*kainē diathēkē*] in [or, "on the basis of"] my blood [*haima*]. Do this, as often as you drink it, in remembrance of me." (RSV)

Provided a person does not insist on harmonizing the two accounts by force, it is obvious that the differences, especially in the second part, are considerable. As to their respective places in the history of the tradition, the older form is that offered by Paul. (I think a consensus among scholars is developing nowadays on this point.) The two most important arguments for the priority of the Pauline version are these:

(1) The phrase "after supper" (*meta to deipnēsai*) in the middle of the Pauline formula allows us to recognize that the two individual actions are thought of as separated from each other. Between them comes the meal. In the account given by Mark, on the other hand, the word over the wine follows immediately after the word over the bread. The impression is given here of a celebration which encompasses only these two parts, placed together and used in reference to one another.

There can be no doubt that, in this respect at least, the formula transmitted by Paul is older. If the Lord's Supper originated on Palestinian soil (we shall go into this matter further later on), then it is embedded in the framework of the Jewish meal. This setting is precisely what has been maintained in the phrase "after supper." But one may also detect the further development. In Corinth the Lord's Supper was celebrated in connection with a meal, most likely at the end of, or after the conclusion of, an ordinary meal where all have eaten their fill (I Cor. 11:17 ff.). Thus the formula which Paul cites contains a vestige even older than the practice in the Corinthian congregation. Two stages are thus observable here. In the first stage (represented in the formula cited by Paul, but pre-Pauline) the two actions are separated by the meal. In the second stage (the actual Corinthian practice) a meal takes place first, then the Lord's Supper occurs as a kind of sacramental appendix or conclusion to the ordinary meal. Consequently the sacramental meal becomes something independent; it is very easy, then, for the phrase "after supper," which has now become superfluous in the formula, to fall away. The Marcan formula is thus shown to be the third stage.

(2) In the so-called second "word of interpretation" (*Deutewort*) there are considerable differences between the formulas that have been transmitted by Paul and Mark.

In Paul it reads: "This cup is the new covenant (*kainē diathēkē*) in (or, "by virtue of") my blood (*haima*)." What stands out here quite clearly is the covenant (*diathēkē*) and not the blood. In outline, the formula runs:

cup = covenant (*diathēkē*);
this covenant is then interpreted further by "blood" (*haima*).

With Mark, on the other hand, the second word goes like this: "This is my blood of the covenant (*haima tēs diathēkēs*)." The emphasis is unambiguously on "blood" (*haima*). However, it is not the cup, but the contents of the cup which is meant. In outline, the formula runs:

contents of the cup = blood (*haima*);
this blood is then interpreted further as blood of the covenant (*haima tēs diathēkēs*).

In Paul, then, we have a cup-covenant-(blood) word, while in Mark, on the other hand, it is a contents-of-the-cup-blood-(covenant) word.

To recover the original form, a comparison with the first "word of interpretation" is helpful. In both the Pauline and Marcan formulations the bread is related to the body (*sōma*). It is to be noted that the Pauline formula is incongruent; in outline it goes like this:

bread = body (*sōma*)
cup = covenant (*diathēkē*).

Contrast the congruence of the Marcan version:

bread = (*sōma*);
contents of the cup = blood (*haima*).

Precisely this observation—even though it is only stylistic—raises the suspicion that in the Marcan formula the incongruence of the Pauline version has been harmonized. At the same time the term "cup" (*potērion*) has been allowed to stand although it no longer fits precisely, for it is no longer the cup, but its contents that is meant.

Later we shall go into this alteration again. For the time being, however, we can, if we combine the latter considerations with the previous ones, offer an initial reason why the Marcan formula has been harmonized: the meal has disappeared, and the two actions are brought together. Then, however, it becomes a matter of corresponding simply to stylistic laws (especially in the case of liturgical texts) that parallel sayings are given parallel wording. As long as the two actions were divided by the meal and kept separate, there was no compelling need for a harmonizing recasting.

This reason (harmonization), by itself, is admittedly hardly enough to explain the recasting of the Marcan formula. Indeed, it is apparently not even the decisive one; for the shift in *emphasis* which appears here is very likely manifestation of a shift in *contents* which has entered into the development and which, on its part, makes the meal itself superfluous. We must now go into this matter.

THE LORD'S SUPPER IN A PRE-PAULINE FORMULA

We begin again with the phrase "after supper" (*meta to deipnēsai*). What we have established is that the Lord's Supper was originally celebrated within the setting of a meal. We can see this from the formula transmitted by Paul. But that means that the two actions of the Lord's Supper did not originally take place one immediately after the other; they were rather separated from one another — even by an interval of time. This point has frequently been noted before. But now we ought to draw the consequences of it. I mention two.

(1) The two actions of the Lord's Supper have to be understood separately. This means that in exegesis one may not argue from their parallelism; rather one should pay attention to the peculiar meaning of each action in its own place.

(2) Not only are we not permitted to start from the parallelism, but we are also required to ask about the relationship of each of the actions to the meal as a whole. For these two actions were originally single components of a total meal and were embedded in it.

In exegesis a decisive — methodological — mistake is often made. We know that *at a later time* the two actions occurred together. However, this knowledge (derived from our practice today and also from the Marcan formula) is then imposed on the formula transmitted by Paul. Whoever does this makes it appear that we are dealing with two isolated acts within the meal and that they alone have significance. But is this allowable? In that case the Pauline formula is being interpreted anachronistically again and again to the degree that one assumes the later development valid for the earlier situation.

In exegesis of the formulas attention must therefore be paid — and this seems to me absolutely necessary methodologically—to the history of the tradition in its temporal sequence. Then one can ask how a later understanding has developed from an earlier statement. Since there has now been established the development from a complete meal to a(n abridged) meal-celebration with (only) two actions which happen one directly after the other, we must leave the later development out of consideration for the time being and—at least for our exegesis of the formula transmitted by Paul—start with the unity of the meal.

Provisionally, therefore, we can draw this conclusion: if the development from the formula cited by Paul to the Marcan formulation consists in a movement from a total meal—somehow qualified—to an abridged cultic meal-celebration, this means that what still remain in Mark (and so also for us) are two excerpts from what was earlier an entire meal. It is now *the two excerpts* which have special importance. But one will have to ask at this point, in view of the fact that the meal has been broken up, whether the meaning of the whole has not at the same time been changed or at least disarranged.

In this connection the form of the word about the cup in the tradition transmitted by Paul now becomes instructive. The cup passed around the congregation is described as "the new covenant (*kainē diathēkē*) by virtue of the blood" of Jesus.

When we now examine this phrase by itself, being careful not to read into the formulation too quickly all that we know from other texts, it becomes impossible to substitute "*contents* of the cup" for "cup." There is no mention of the contents. Note further that the "interpretation" refers to the covenant (*diathēkē*) and not to the blood (*haima*); the latter serves rather to define the covenant more exactly. There can be no doubt: it is not an "element" that is interpreted here but the cup, which at the meal passes around the table and from which all partici-pants in the meal drink. Of this cup, which makes the circle around the table, it is said, "This is the new covenant." This is the new, i.e., the eschatological, covenant instituted by God.

But that means that, in this participation in the cup, the celebrating congregation has a share in the new covenant; it actualizes this new covenant; yes, one might even go so far as to say that in this sharing in the cup, the celebrating congregation "is" the "new covenant." But the community is this, as the interpretative addition shows, on the basis of the blood of Christ, that is, by virtue of his death, which is understood here as the basis, the inauguration, of the new covenant.

Thus the word over the cup has an *ecclesiological* character, the ecclesiological assertion being rooted in Christology. The whole, however, is presented as an eschatological *action* (*Vollzug*) for the very reason that the new covenant "is actualized" (*vollzieht*) by the sharing of the cup. But its validity and basis are in the death of Christ.

We turn now to the word over the bread. It is commonly asserted that here there is a sacramental *communio* — namely, that those who *eat* the bread partake of the *body* of Christ — and that this happens just because they consume the bread (which is taken as tantamount to saying, "because they eat the 'body of Christ'").

It is a peculiar fact, however, that the *formula* says absolutely nothing about *eating*. It does not even say anything about the bread's being *given*. Both these details are read all too easily into the passage out of Marcan and Matthean formulas, although, of course, one rightly assumes that the bread is to be eaten.

It is just for that reason that care should again be taken not to harmonize things too quickly; or, to put it more exactly, we should take care not to commit the anachronism of interpreting the earlier formula by the later one. In the early formula precisely this omission is striking — the absence of terminology connected with *eating* and *distribution*. Surely this is no accident. Regardless of how certain we may be that bread was to be eaten, the absence of such terminology raises the question: What really is being "interpreted" here?

If we examine the plain words and make no assumptions about things being meant which are not actually said, there are the following possibilities as to what is being interpreted: the taking of the bread, the thanksgiving, or the breaking of the bread (but *not* the distribution of the bread or the bread itself, for about these the text says nothing).

We warned above against making the too hasty assumption that the two actions, eating and drinking, are parallel. If we heed this admonition, we are not permitted to argue that, since in the word over the cup it is not an element that is interpreted, the same must be true of the word over the bread. Nevertheless, when the wording by itself shows this, then the correspondence with the word over the cup becomes corroborative evidence. In the word over the bread, too, it is not an "element," not the bread, that is being interpreted.

That this was actually the original meaning, there is evidence (in addition to the wording of the formula at I Corinthians 11:24–25) in I Corinthians 10:16–17; the evidence is indirect but still convincing.

In verse 16 Paul is repeating the tradition of the Christian community which he can assume is known in Corinth. The entire context shows this. In verse 15 Paul says that he speaks as to "sensible men." He asks the Corinthians themselves to judge what he says. He is thus reminding them of something already known, of something that was part of the tradition transmitted to them.

Admittedly, Paul cites the tradition (note again the parallelism of the formula) as a question and not as an assertion, but that is due to the context. Verse 16 says simply: "The cup of blessing which we *bless* [observe that it does not say, 'whose contents we drink'], is it not a par-ticipation [*koinōnia*] in the blood [= the sacrificial death] of Christ? The bread which we *break* [note that it does not say, 'the bread which we eat'], is it not a participation in the body of Christ [*sōma Christou*]?"

Then, from verse 17 on, we have a Pauline interpretation of the pre-Pauline formula: "Because there is one bread, we who are many are one body, for we all partake of the one bread." This verse makes clear the following: Paul in I Corinthians—precisely also in this connection, in view of the misunderstandings in Corinth—is concerned to emphasize the unity of the congregation. Paul demonstrates this unity in the one-ness of the bread. (It is in accord with this concern that in the liturgical text, verse 16, Paul has mentioned the cup before the bread.) Verse 17 then further makes clear that what is at issue is a partaking (*koinōnia, Teilhabe*) which is actualized, according to Paul, by participation (*Teilnahme*) in the table fellowship.

The decisive question here is still, What is interpreted? What is explained? Our text says unequivocally: "The cup which we *bless* [i.e., over which we utter our thanksgiving prayer] . . . the bread which we *break* [again this means, over which we speak our thanksgiving prayer]." The thanksgiving takes place at the breaking of bread. This is in harmony with Jewish custom, and there is evidence that "breaking of bread" (*klasis tou artou* or *klan arton*) is a technical term for saying the prayer of thanksgiving.

We find the same emphases, then, in I Corinthians 10:16 and in the formula transmitted by Paul in chapter 11, and in both instances we are dealing with pre-Pauline formulations which he has taken over. Termi-nology connected with eating is lacking. It is not the food that is inter-preted; rather it is clear that the fellowship is constituted at the meal. It is this fellowship which is described as a "new covenant" (*kainē diathēkē*) or as "the body," namely, the body of Christ. These two expressions, however, are basically equivalent in meaning; their difference is that one uses Jewish, the other Hellenistic, terminology.

We shall return to Paul in a moment, but first let us ask if there is anything else that we can find out from the formula he took over. If we keep in mind that what originally characterized the Lord's Supper was the unity of the whole common meal, it is clear that the breaking of the bread and the blessing of the cup are in fact the "liturgical" places in this common meal. That means that at these two points, at the breaking and the blessing, there is an explicit formulation about what the whole common meal signifies, or what it is. Within the framework of a meal, during a complete meal, there are two particular places — and precisely at the "liturgical" places — where interpretative statements are made about what this meal is and what the group is which eats the meal: the group which is celebrating, praying, and giving thanks is "the body of Christ"; as such it is actualizing "the new covenant."

THE LORD'S SUPPER IN PAUL AND MARK

We return now to Paul himself, who takes the development one step further.

I said earlier that in Corinth the Lord's Supper was still celebrated in connection with an ordinary meal, but apparently at the end of the meal. This we may deduce from the perversions in Corinth, which Paul criticizes (I Cor. 11:21-22). When the congregation gathers, right away they start to eat. Those who come late find people who are drunk. The Corinthians may have been of the opinion that this was not so bad, since those who came late were not missing anything, because they could still participate in the "communion" (*Abendmahl*). But Paul says that what they then celebrate is no longer a Lord's Supper. These perversions could have arisen only when the cultic celebration had been shoved back to the end of the meal. To *this* practice Paul does not object. He thus assumes that the "cultic" celebration is already distinct from the meal as a whole.

At still another point Paul goes a step beyond the earlier tradition. It can be shown that it is he who for the first time speaks expressly of eating and drinking. In 10:21, for example, he speaks of "drinking the cup of the Lord," and in 11:26-27, where he paraphrases the action at the celebration of the Lord's Supper, once again it is Paul who makes explicit mention of eating the bread and drinking the cup, points on which the formula itself is silent.

This means that Paul now expressly includes what was indeed implicit in the formula but had not yet been stated or even emphasized, namely, eating and drinking. However, even here it is not as though Paul were talking about the food as such; what is at issue is the *partaking* which is *actualized at the eating*. The crucial question is this: Participation in the cup of demons—or in the cup of the Lord?

That Paul represents in this sense an independent, intermediate step in the interpretation of the Lord's Supper is shown by his dispute with the problems in the Corinthian congregation. The "strong," who are of the opinion that they can participate in sacrificial meals consecrated to idols without harm to their Christianity, are criticized by Paul on the grounds that the two forms of participation, the sacrificial meal for idols and the Lord's Supper of the Christian community, are mutually exclusive acts. The strong in Corinth have apparently not perceived that the act of participating in table fellowship has "sacramental reality" (I Cor. 10:14 ff.). They derive the freedom for this behavior from their Christian knowledge that the idols to whom the offering is made are in reality no gods at all, but rather "nothings." Thus for these "strong" Christians the meat that is offered to idols is only that—meat. On the other side, the "weak" take offense at the *consumption* of the *meat*. They would scarcely have participated in sacrificial meals consecrated to idols. Rather they faced such questions as whether to buy meat at the market place which came from slaughterings in pagan cult, and whether to eat such meat at secular, purely social meals. Hence they evidently believed in an actual *material* communication of the demonic through such sacrificial meat. Paul rejects that notion outright, and yet enjoins consideration for the weak for the sake of love (I Cor. 8:1 ff.). It is clear, then, that Paul sees the sacramental reality in the *act of table fellowship*, whether with demons or with the Lord.

Thus the way is prepared for a development which is more readily discerned at a later stage, namely in Mark. We may recall that the biggest difference between the cultic formulas in Paul and in Mark appears in the so-called second "word of interpretation": the saying about cup and covenant becomes a saying about the contents of the cup (wine) and blood. I said earlier that this is an attempt to harmonize the second word of interpretation with the first, but I also noted that this harmonizing is not the only, and probably not the decisive, reason for the reshaping of the second word of interpretation.

What is striking at this point is that in Mark we again find the terminology about eating which was still missing from the formula received by Paul and which is encountered first in the use he makes of the formula. Added to the Marcan saying about the bread ("he took bread, gave thanks, and broke it") is the comment, "and *gave* it to them," an emphasis which is further underscored by the imperative that follows, "take" (*labete*). The shift of emphasis is unmistakable. The Pauline formula puts the stress on the thanksgiving said *at* the breaking of the bread; the Marcan formula dwells on the *giving* and *taking of the bread over which a thanksgiving has been said*. Similarly, in the second word of interpretation, the Pauline formula puts the stress on the cup, while the Marcan formula adds, "He *gave* it to them, and they all *drank* of it." It is consistent with this that attention is drawn to the *blood* (of the covenant); emphasis is put on the *contents* of the cup. Naturally, the contents cannot be described as a "new covenant"; and just for that reason it is not emphasized. There is a shift in emphasis which is not merely the result of an attempt to make the second word of interpretation similar to the first; what is decisive is that something different is being interpreted, namely, the "elements" which are consumed. Furthermore, since the phrase "after supper" in the formula has now become superfluous, it is dropped; the two actions of eating and drinking occur together and are naturally intended to share a common interpretation. "Body and blood" are now the two "components" of the Christ who gave himself in death.

Thus sacramental reality is now attached to the elements, to that which is consumed. This feature was not yet present in Paul; there is not a trace of it in the formula which he transmits. Had the formula there connected body and blood, the term "body" (*sōma*) would hardly have been used, but, rather, "flesh" (*sarx*) since "flesh and blood" (*sarx kai haima*) are the "whole man."

Let us summarize what we have said so far. It is possible to speak of a development within the primitive Christian community of its celebration and practice of the Lord's Supper. This development has been traced from its pre-Pauline to its Marcan form. At the outset the meaning for the entire meal was expressed at places which were already liturgical. Later the actual meal was omitted. With Paul it is still a matter of having a meal, but the action is tied to eating bread and drinking wine. In the Marcan formula, finally, what is asserted is related explicitly to the food, which is understood as the "body and blood of Christ."

It should immediately be clear how extremely difficult it is, on the basis of these exegetical findings on the history of the tradition, to systematize the differing presentations within the New Testament and go on to dogmatic assertions which might help us today in understanding our celebration of the Lord's Supper.

Jesus and the Lord's Supper

Is it now possible, however, to take that segment of the development of the Lord's Supper which we have considered thus far and set it into the total development in the New Testament, in order to push back historically a step further? Above all, we need to determine if it is possible to push back from the formula given by Paul to an even earlier stage. The matter becomes ever so much more difficult because we do not have older formulas and must depend in part upon indirect sources.

Specifically, therefore, the question is, Where does the Pauline formula come from? As we push back, do we get to the institution of the Lord's Supper by Jesus?

We may observe, for a starter, that the Pauline formula begins with the phrase "on the night when the Lord Jesus was betrayed." That phrase, however, does not really settle the historical question. It fails to do so (even if we take for granted that the institution took place on the night of the betrayal), because we are still not told what was instituted at that time. Although the phrase "on the night (of the betrayal)" is lacking in the Marcan formula, it is nonetheless implicitly there, too, through the insertion of this cultic formula into the passion history. In that case, however, Jesus, according to the Marcan formula, would have instituted something quite different from what the Pauline formula maintains. But even in Paul's formula there are features present which one could hardly refer back to Jesus. One such example would be the ecclesiological character of the formula, in particular the term "body" (*sōma*). The description of the church as "body" of Christ is Hellenistic, not Palestinian. Further, the founding of "the new covenant" through the blood of Jesus as the date for the founding of the church points to a later period. Thus, even if one wants to speak of an institution by Jesus of a celebration which is to be continued, we are faced with the problem of finding out what content such a celebration might have had.

One must keep this problem very clearly in mind, and then, surely, one will be able to come to terms with its solution. If one speaks about an institution of the Lord's Supper by Jesus, if one intends thereby to affirm that Jesus did institute the Lord's Supper, then this affirmation really does not say anything as long as one does not, or cannot, state what it was that was instituted. If one cannot establish the *contents* of what was instituted, then his affirmation merely remains: Jesus instituted a rite.

But what does that say if at the same time one must affirm that we know the contents of this rite only in formulations which cannot come from Jesus—since he did not think in Hellenistic terms? We would be faced, then, with these two affirmations: Jesus instituted a rite; the content of this rite was later on stated by the Christian community in different ways. This can only lead to the judgment that we cannot state the actual content of what Jesus instituted.

Now since the contents were stated by the early church, but these contents differ, at the least the question ought to be posed here whether in the Pauline formula the indication of time ("on the night when he was betrayed") might not also belong to the contents of the post-Easter formula and thus be intended as a *theological* interpretation. In that case we would be dealing with an "etiology," which makes sense only when understood theologically: the early church knew and said that with the cross something new had begun; therefore it carried back its celebration not just in a general way to Jesus, but specifically to the day of his crucifixion.

There are still other arguments which make it seem doubtful that the formula's time indication is to be understood historically. To all appearances, there was a passion history which did not include the cultic formula, as is made clear by a literary analysis of Mark 14. In that case, however, question arises whether such a passion history (without "Words of Institution") is readily conceivable if Jesus actually instituted the Lord's Supper on the night of his betrayal. If such were the case, if Jesus at that time had instituted a celebration which was to be repeated, therefore a cult, then one would also suppose that not only would that Lord's Supper be celebrated, but that its origin would be known, too. But then, when the passion history was edited (in its pre-Marcan form) would the Lord's Supper have been passed over? This is hardly thinkable.

On the other hand, however, it is quite understandable that a Lord's Supper whose origin was not tied essentially to this date would not be mentioned in the passion history. Thus, the findings of a literary investigation of the passion history cast doubt on the historicity of the institution of the Lord's Supper.

Another consideration appears even weightier. I have already indicated that Jesus was concerned with an anticipation of the future, that *now* the future is being actualized. But with him there is no apocalyptic speculation. He is not interested in the future as such. Further, we find no indication that Jesus thought at all about institutionalizing his anticipation of the future. We find no indication that he intended something like a church.

Not to be misunderstood, let me add immediately that this sentence should in no case be turned around. That Jesus did not intend something like a church in no way means that the later rise of a church absolutely had to contradict his intention. All that we mean to say is that the problem of a future church lay outside Jesus' reflections. This conclusion—a historical one—can be made with great assurance on the basis of our sources.

But if the problem of the church lay outside the range of Jesus' reflection, so also must the institution of a cult for this church.

Before I go on to give another reason for my position on the dating as theological, not historical, let me first summarize. Two aspects which we have studied make a positive answer to the question about institution of the Lord's Supper uncertain, if not precarious. It is extremely difficult to refer the contents of the Pauline formula back to Jesus; and in the face of all that we can ascertain about the preaching and activity of Jesus, it is still less likely to assume institution of a cult by Jesus. Thus the supposition that Jesus instituted this Lord's Supper on the eve of his death poses so many difficulties that the careful historian must put more than just a question mark here.

One thing must remain clear: whether Jesus instituted a cult, and what content this cult had, can only be answered by the method of historical investigation. Under no circumstances may faith take the place of historical knowledge. To be sure, the answer that we get, then, is "only" a historical answer. If the early church at a later time referred its celebration back to the night of the betrayal, a theological assertion is there present — more exactly, a theological interpretation of its cult is present there. This interpretation, however, fits well with the tendency in the development of early Christian assertions. There are several examples of a chronological reference being used in order to make a theological (but not historical!) assertion. Precisely this applies also in the case of Jesus' death and the Lord's Supper.

According to the Fourth Gospel, Jesus died on the day of Preparation for the Passover (18:28; 19:31, 42), and in fact at the very hour when the lambs were being slaughtered at the temple. What is asserted in this synchronization is clear: Jesus is the "true" Passover lamb (cf. I Cor. 5:7). According to the Synoptics, Jesus died one day later, but held a "Christian Lord's Supper" at the time when the Jews were holding their Passover meal (Mark 14:12 ff.). The assertion here must therefore be: the Christian Lord's Supper is the true Passover meal.

It is significant that these two datings cannot be harmonized historically. Either Jesus died on Nisan 14 (the day of Preparation) or on Nisan 15 (Passover). But if one sees that it is not a matter of historical, but of theological, assertions which are made with the help of (diverse!) datings, then the difficulties so often found between the Synoptics, on the one hand, and the Gospel of John, on the other, disappear with the realization that theological statements have been historicized.

When it is realized that "dating" is used in this way, thus making it very unlikely to speak of an institution of the Lord's Supper by Jesus, then the "dating" in the Pauline formula, too, poses historically no difficulty anymore.

Further evidence for our assumption is given — in its way — by the Fourth Gospel. There, too, the Lord's Supper is traced back to Jesus. Of course, it is not put at a definite time, but it is localized in the life of Jesus when in the sixth chapter he who has come in the flesh (*sarx*) gives a discourse on the Lord's Supper. Thus the Fourth Gospel shows that a dating on the night of the betrayal was apparently not universally connected with the existence of the Lord's Supper as a Christian celebration. If that were the case, the evangelist could scarcely have decided not to put it in chapter 13. (If one makes the assumption, which is likely, of an ecclesiastical redactor for the Gospel of John, the argument is shifted only slightly; what is then striking is that the redactor puts the Lord's Supper into chapter 6 and not chapter 13.)

Thus there is much that speaks against counting on a historical institution of the Lord's Supper by Jesus. An immediate warning must be issued, however, not to draw overhasty conclusions here. Such a thing happens when, solely on the basis of the findings made so far, the accounts of the institution of the Lord's Supper are described as "etiological cult legends." One cannot deny that such an ascription accords well with the historical findings, but certain distinctions have to be made here.

If one indeed assumed that the Lord's Supper originated somewhere in the early post-Easter church—very likely on Hellenistic soil where such cult meals were already known—and if the early church itself now developed a meal analogous to such sacred meals, which it *then* referred back etiologically to an institution by Jesus, then one might describe the account of the institution as an etiological cult legend in the proper sense of the word.

But this is by no means our only alternative. This point must very much be kept in mind: one cannot draw the conclusion from the tendency toward historicizing—dating the cult for the purpose of theological interpretation—that this cult arose only later, i.e., after the (theological!) "date" given.

Ignoring this impulse toward historicizing and etiology, ignoring also the emphasis on "institution" which accompanies it, we must therefore attempt to get at *the* Lord's Supper which existed *before* this historicizing set in. Naturally, we should realize that we are getting into an area the tradition-history of which is not easy to survey. Nevertheless, the question does not seem to me to be hopeless, for there are several clues, and we find some leads which are worth tracking down.

It has often been pointed out, for example, that the accounts of feeding miracles in the Gospels contain Lord's Supper terminology. The question of immediate dependence can be kept open and is not even that decisive, in view of the fact that the Jewish meal provides the common basis for terminology of both these feedings and the Lord's Supper. The Jewish meal itself often plays a role in the Gospels. We hear about table fellowship with Jesus. He is described as the "bridegroom." What this presupposes is that the eschatological meal—the meal of the consummation—is pictured as a wedding feast. If Jesus is called bridegroom, he is thereby described as the head of the house at this eschatological meal. But this means that we are dealing with considered Christology: the meal which Jesus had on earth with his followers is understood as an eschatological meal (Christology in action!); and out of it grows (upon reflection) the assertion "Jesus is the bridegroom."

Light is now thrown also on the other scenes involving meals which the tradition gives us. We hear about meals where tax collectors and sinners are the table companions, that is to say, people who are considered cultically unclean. Keep in mind that the meal played quite a different role for the Jews than for us. Their precise regulations about food indicate this. Furthermore, remember that every Jewish meal — already by virtue of the very prayers that are spoken at the beginning and at its conclusion — is a "cultic" meal. That fact accords very well with another concept already mentioned, namely, that fulfillment in the kingdom of God is often thought of as a table fellowship. When you put all this together, the eschatological perspective becomes clear in which the early church saw these meals of Jesus.

This impression of the meals held by Jesus dovetails well with the impression witnesses had of Jesus' life and words. This becomes very clear when several assertions are put together:

(a) In the encounter with Jesus men are brought to faith.

(b) In the encounter with Jesus (in the reaction of men toward him) the eschatological decision at the judgment is already pronounced.

(c) In the encounter with Jesus (in table fellowship) the consummation, the eschaton, is anticipated.

(d) The *function* of Jesus is always shown in exactly the same structure. In eating and drinking with Jesus, the participants experience a fellowship which they assert to be a foretaste of the eschatological fellowship.

When one sees this, it also becomes apparent that these meals of Jesus are understood as an offer, as a gift. That comes out most clearly where tax collectors and sinners are invited — people who otherwise do not "belong." Here the notion of "offer" clearly comes out, especially in view of the people who are invited: the sharper the contrast (and tax collectors and sinners are right at the bottom), the more sharply the gift stands out. This notion of gift, then, appears with particular clarity in the accounts about feeding miracles: immeasurable, unlimited is that which Jesus offers as a gift.

We may sum this up by saying that the early church celebrated meals; but the Synoptic tradition shows that already with the earthly Jesus, the meal played a special role. What is transmitted by the tradition belongs to the area of Christology in action. This means, it is not just accounts of any meal which are being transmitted, but those in the action of which Jesus' function is brought out, in the action of which the eschaton is now already realized. This is how far you can come with the analytical method!

THE POST-EASTER CHURCH

The question now arises whether we have found here the initial impulse that set in motion a development which led to the Lord's Supper of the church. Our assignment is to go in the reverse direction, mapping the road, reconstructively, from the oldest meal traditions to the meals in the early church; at the same time this will provide a test for our analysis.

One thing here can be acknowledged to be as good as certain, namely, that after Easter the community continued to celebrate meals; according to Acts 2, they did so with joy (*agalliasis*). Furthermore, the community which celebrated these meals now saw itself (because of the cross and Easter) as the eschatological community, as the community of the new covenant. They celebrated these meals in their homes—as complete meals. That is not only easily understandable, it is also quite natural. There were no Christian worship services yet, but there was a Christian community. Even though the Palestinian, especially the Jerusalem, community still preserved some kind of tie with the temple (or resumed one again), they could scarcely gather there as a *Christian* community. Consequently, they gathered together in that manner in which their fellowship and solidarity were expressed most distinctively: at the common meal.

With these meals the Jesus-tradition was continued. Since Easter they knew him to be alive; they knew him to be present at these meals. Thus the assertions implicit in these meals I should like to call "ecclesiology in action." At the meal the Christian community was *actualized* as the eschatological community.

That which the congregation now experiences at these meals, how they understand them and at the same time how they understand themselves, is given expression, it is formulated. Thus the "contents" of this meal becomes explicit.

In this, something happens that corresponds exactly to the transition from a Christology in action to a considered Christology: what it means to eat together—the action of the meal—is considered and interpreted.

Let us examine these interpretations. In the Pauline formula one can see that at first it is the action itself that is asserted. Now the places become important where this happens — in connection with the prayers at the beginning and at the end of the meal. These two places happen to be opportune for such interpretations. They were the "liturgical" places. It was here that something was already spoken anyhow, something spoken which was fitting. At these points in Jewish (festival) meals Yahweh's saving activities were recalled — an *anamnēsis,* as it were — by reason of which those who celebrated could and did consider themselves to belong to the covenant, to God's people. What is striking about these Jewish prayers is the "ecclesiological" character, so to speak, of these meals which is here asserted and which characterizes those who participate in the meal as belonging to the covenant. It was in an environment of this sort that the Palestinian church lived. At these two places (the breaking of bread, blessing the cup) the Palestinian community was acquainted with interpretations of the meal and of the table fellowship. It is quite natural, then, that at these two places, where something liturgical was usually said, new interpretations were now attached when Jesus' meals were continued.

It is immediately obvious that it is not just these two places as such which are elucidated; instead it is the *total* meal which is interpreted, as well as the *community* which holds the meal. That the interpretations would continue at precisely these two places will be significant for later development and of great consequence.

Reflection begins when the action finds expression by being interpreted; the action is verbalized. The celebrating community *is* the body of Christ, it *is* the new divine establishment (*kainē diathēkē*); and this is *actualized* in the action of the meal. Expression is given to this at the prayer of thanksgiving over the bread at the beginning, and over the cup of blessing at the end, of the meal.

This ecclesiology in action, which has thus been given expression in words, is carried further in the process of reflection, however, in that Christology is now brought in. A reason is offered why the community may regard itself as the eschatological community: it may do so on the basis, or by virtue, of Christ's blood, on the basis of his death on the cross understood as an atoning sacrifice.

It is this stage in the development which is shown in the formula transmitted by Paul — an ecclesiology in action which, upon reflection, finds initial expression and is given christological support.

The transition to Mark has already been described. The centers of gravity have now shifted; what had been items of interpretation receive their own weight.

Precisely the same thing can be observed elsewhere. If, in considered Christology, Jesus is called the Son of God, that very expression takes on its own significance as *it* carries christological development further. Consequently, if Jesus *was* the Son of God, this ascription must (or can) be inserted into other contexts; it can be expressed by the concept of the Virgin Birth, by preexistence, or, on Jewish soil, by the development of adoptionistic ideas.

Something that corresponds exactly happens in the tradition about the Lord's Supper. The christological emphasis, which earlier served to support the ecclesiological, is itself developed.

The concept of "body" is transferred to the bread, which is broken; analogously, the cup's *content* is related to the blood of Christ. Body and blood (that is to say, the whole man) now belong together with bread and wine. The "elements" make their appearance. The presence of the Lord is attached to *this* food. But the meal, which originally stood in the center as the meal of the new covenant, is now robbed of its significance. Hence it is only a logical development that the meal as such is dropped. There remain only the two high points of the meal which were emphasized by the initial interpretation. But in exact correspondence to this, terminology about "eating," which was earlier lacking, now enters into the formula.

The initial reflection is thus continued and in a manner that corresponds exactly to the development in Christology which we have encountered: the action is reflected upon; the action which has been reflected on becomes the object of further reflection, the point of which is to say something about the author of the action (Jesus).

It is the same way with the Lord's Supper: the action is first reflected upon; the action which has been given such consideration becomes the object of further reflection, the point of which is to say something now about the food.

DEVELOPMENT IN THE HELLENISTIC WORLD

Here another important point must be made. This further reflection is done on Hellenistic soil; understandably, Hellenistic concepts are employed for interpretation of the Lord's Supper. Noteworthy in this context is the fact that in Hellenistic thought the communication of the "divine" to men is always portrayed or thought of as material. Thus, for example, "spirit" (*pneuma*) is thought of as "extremely fine matter."

This represents a considerable difference from Jewish thought and Jewish concepts. The Jew thinks historically in that the eschaton becomes for him a present reality by representation or by anticipation. Passover concepts are a good example of this. In the Passover ritual every generation is told to celebrate the festival as if it had itself come out of Egypt. The Exodus of the past is celebrated today. This has nothing at all to do with our modern memorial celebrations; it is a co-celebrating (*mitfeiern*), at which there is a "repeating" of that event so as to bring the past into the present. Among other ways, this comes out very clearly in the effort to make the "repetition" of the celebration imitate as much as possible the original event. The past is "re-presented." Correspondingly, the future is anticipated, perhaps in a meal, in concepts and representation of the Feast of Tabernacles, etc.

This peculiar way of thinking about time—or, to put it more exactly, this peculiar *experiencing* of time (which can be seen, for example, in the form of the Hebrew tenses, which strike us as strange)—determined the celebrations of the Palestinian church. Through re-presentation they celebrated the table fellowships with Jesus and at the same time in them anticipated the consummation as the community of the new, the eschatological, covenant.

It was entirely different on the Hellenistic scene. There the "divine" (one can no longer really speak of an eschaton) is imparted by material means. It was these materialistic categories which were used to express in a way appropriate to Hellenism what in the Palestinian milieu was expressed by temporal categories or was temporally experienced.

That the Corinthians could not properly have made do with the Lord's Supper as set forth in the formula transmitted by Paul is quite evident, for the formula implied nothing else but that they were to celebrate a meal according to Jewish customs. Instead, customs at meals usual in their world entered in. Features characteristic of the Jewish meal were moved to the end of the entire meal. Apparently, eating bread and drinking wine were understood as the reception of sacramental elements. For the outlook of "the weak," this is as good as certain; for "the strong," it is at least very likely. (The freedom which the strong showed with regard to meat offered to idols was theologically conditioned by "de-divinization" of the demons, but this does not necessarily mean that they surrendered completely their belief in a material impartation of the divine.)

Paul does not polemicize against the Corinthians' accommodation of Jewish meal customs to practices common to their world, an adaptation which resulted in shifting the liturgical acts to the end of the meal. What he does polemicize against is that in this way the fellowship aspect of the meal is lost, that is to say, precisely that which was essential for the original communion (*Abendmahl*). But it was this original communion which the Corinthians could not celebrate because for them the meal was in itself a social meal and not really a cultic event. For them the cultic was the abbreviated meal-celebration shifted to the end. Thus communion was only an abbreviated liturgical act.

It was only here, therefore, that Paul could still attach an argument. Since the meal held at the beginning by the Corinthians was only a *social* meal without any specific cultic character, Paul had to begin simply with these isolated liturgical features at the end. But once again he is concerned apparently with the *action* as such of this abbreviated celebratory meal, which consisted now only of eating and drinking bread and wine.

This situation would seem to make the contrasts very clear. That confrontation between Jewish and Hellenistic thought which is of so much consequence for the Lord's Supper begins its last stage here.

Thus we must say that the slow emergence of emphasis on the elements and their significance is Hellenistic interpretation of the original Palestinian meal. That means, we have to do with features which are already interpretations (*Interpretamente*) and not with the content (*Sache*) itself. Eating holy food is not the real issue; rather it is already an interpretation of the matter, one which—as an interpretation—had its home on Hellenistic soil.

It has sometimes been said that the Lord's Supper was derived from the religious environment of early Christianity. That is probably false. But items of interpretation (*Interpretamente*) were taken from there. And this is something entirely different! For where an interpretation comes from is relatively unimportant as long as it is in a position to express, to some extent, the contents of that which is being interpreted (in this case, the contents of the meal). We must emphasize the phrase "to some extent," for an interpretation never fits exactly the thing itself;

but above all, an interpretation is really understandable and effective only where people think in the categories from which the interpretation derives. Surely, an interpretation is necessary where the old categories are no longer understandable. It was necessary, then, for the "Hellenists" to express the reality of the meal in a different way than happened on Palestinian soil.

This freedom in interpretation also deserves attention. From it an interesting light is cast on discussion about the Lord's Supper in recent years—and centuries. It seems quite clear that the question, Is it "holy food" or not? was in no way involved in the original Lord's Supper. To be sure, the discussion between Lutherans and Reformed cannot simply be limited to the question whether "is" or "means" is the correct term. The subject is much more complex. But it can be helpful if—in order to accentuate just one aspect of this knotty issue—we concentrate for a moment on this abbreviated way of putting the problem. In this case it becomes plain at once that this debate is not over the thing itself, but over what is already an interpretation.

What we discover is simply this: if a person interprets historically (that is, if he asks in accord with the Hellenistic understanding of this interpretation), then the term "is" turns out to be right. But for the word "signifies," no stage in the tradition gives support, not even the Palestinian, for there they were still not at all concerned with the "elements."

It should be clear, however, that to regard the term "is" as a formulation legitimate for dogmatic theology would be a hasty conclusion, for it is not permissible to take *one* interpretation—one that is not only secondary, but even a chance interpretation with respect to the categories employed—and to exalt it to the level of a dogmatic statement.

The systematic-dogmatic considerations must begin at another point. We shall go into this later.

After Paul and Mark

But now we must pursue the development of concepts of the Lord's Supper a bit further by the tradition-history method.

We said that in the Pauline *formula* (and this is true also for I Corinthians 10:16) we are dealing with an initial interpretation of an *action*. The Pauline *context* in which it is set provides the transition to a later development, in that here terminology about *eating* is introduced.

The Marcan formula goes a step further. We said earlier that here the presence of the Lord is attached to the food, and thus the "elements" come into view. That statement must now be somewhat modified. It is true that here bread and the contents of the cup are "interpreted." However, this does not happen in isolation, but in conjunction with the consumption of these "elements." That becomes clear particularly with the word over the cup, for there is a statement about what the wine "is" only after it has been reported that they "all drank of it." If we want to make clear this further development in contrast to the Pauline practice, we could perhaps express it by saying that the gift of the action is not asserted by the action in a general way, but is now associated exclusively with the bread and the wine and is conveyed by *consuming* these *elements*.

In this way the event is much more "materialized" than was — so far as terminological indications go — the case with Paul. And it was precisely this sort of development which continued.

When the meal is omitted, the ecclesiological aspect, the character of the Lord's Supper as the meal of the eschatological community, retreats into the background. At any rate, this feature is no longer *immediately* present; it is also no longer constitutive. The food becomes "the medicine of immortality" (*pharmakon athanasias*) according to Ignatius, *Epistle to the Ephesians* 20:2, or the antidote to death. It contains the powers of the other world.

Now the eschatological community has become the *cultic* community. Soon, the food is no longer partaken of at a table but received at an altar which one must approach. Hand in hand with this, the development of the notion of "office" occurs. One can even take the food (as holy food) to the sick who could not be present at the church service.

Thus a development can indeed be traced in which, by a kind of logical necessity, one stage follows another, and one can recognize a development (and that is the thesis stated in the Prologue) which runs almost exactly parallel to that of Christology — the action is asserted, then the action is reflected on, finally he who performs the action is, upon reflection, given explication. At those points in the christological development where we find assertions of explicit Christology, here, in the development of the Lord's Supper, we find assertions about the "elements," which, in fact, have christological functions as "bearers" of the gift.

Christological development began with, or shortly after, Easter and was completed relatively soon thereafter. Hence, the parallel development in the Lord's Supper, which also was completed relatively rapidly, is not really astonishing. It simply could not be argued that such a rapid development and transformation of the Lord's Supper is unthinkable. For the development of Christology, which is just as rapid, is easily demonstrable.

There is, of course, still one point that deserves our more precise attention. In spite of the parallel development there is also a characteristic difference. An interpretation never fully expresses adequately the thing which it interprets. An explicit Christology which attempts to express the eschatological function of Jesus (which is manifested in action) and which tries to express this in terms of person (as, for example, by the application of titles) always says less than that which was set forth by the "Christology in action." Furthermore, such titles are themselves useful only within limits—only in the environment where they arise and in which they are understood. That is why explication is always at the same time a narrowing-down. To be sure, it is possible for different explications to stand alongside each other. Then what results are different Christologies, which simply cannot be harmonized but which, just because they are explications, can point back, each in its own way, to the original complex representation in the action.

It is completely different, however, with the Lord's Supper. *One* explication has been developed further. But this means that each new stage represents a further departure from the one which preceded. At the beginning stood the meal as an eschatological event. This meal is interpreted at two points. Then these two points are lifted out of the entire meal complex. The interpretation goes on but is now related only to what happened at these two points—consuming bread and wine. Finally, the bread and wine are themselves interpreted; and this interpretation is expanded christologically.

HISTORICAL DEVELOPMENT AND CELEBRATION TODAY

Before we go further into this matter, another consideration must be inserted. The formula transmitted by Paul is probably of Palestinian origin. But if the Hellenistic notion of the "body of Christ" (*sōma Christou*) lies behind the ecclesiological assertion in the word over the bread, we are here confronted by a Hellenization which was not yet, or at least not primarily, oriented to materialistic categories. This concept could not have been part of the original Palestinian formula. What earlier concept it suppressed or replaced can at best only be surmised since it remains necessarily uncertain.

On the other hand, a person might, with some assurance, say that the formula transmitted by Paul was shaped in an environment where both Jewish and Hellenistic thought were current. That was the case, for example, in Antioch. Jewish meal customs still lived on there, and at the same time there was contact with the culture of Hellenism. The experience of cultic meal fellowship could then be expressed as well by the concept of the new covenant as by the notion of a (collective) body (*sōma*). The latter lay ready at hand in the Hellenistic environment, originating in religious thought where it expressed the inner tie of the cultic fellowship with its Redeemer. Thus both the word over the cup and the bread-word have an ecclesiological character.

The reason that both assertions are possible is, however, the Jewish meal with its cultic communal character. If the Lord's Supper moves into another cultural environment where meals are understood differently, these assertions must necessarily become incomprehensible. And that is just what happened in Corinth. The difficulty was mastered by holding, at the end of a social meal, an abbreviated, liturgical meal-celebration, which, however, had to be understood now in a different way. No longer could the action as such be decisive, but rather the material communication of divine reality.

As a matter of fact, then it is a torso that is left, namely, the real presence of the *Kyrios* in the holy food. It cannot be denied that here a decisive turn has been made. At the outset, too, there had been a kind of "real presence," though not one at a set place or tied to certain elements. It was not even, properly speaking, a real presence of the *Kyrios,* but the presence in the community of the eschaton which was actualized by the *Kyrios.*

This quality of "eschatological existence," which was expressed by members being together at a common meal, was lost. The "table of the Lord" is no longer a table around which people sit and at which the new covenant established by Jesus is realized by being together at the meal; rather, it has become a table to sit in front of or to approach.

Precisely this is what has survived down to the present. Hence two things need to be said. We are faced, on the one hand, with a development which is in itself very understandable throughout, but which is marked by historical contingency which ought not to be overlooked. If Christianity had not been transmitted to us through Hellenism, these categories in connection with the Lord's Supper would not have cropped up. Yet one could hardly maintain that the "content" would nevertheless not have survived—admittedly, though, with the help of other interpretive materials. Thus if the fortuitous history of our Lord's Supper tradition is, on the one hand, plain, so also, on the other hand, it needs to be pointed out that further continued interpretation seriously reduced the complex "content" of the original.

But this means that Jesus did not at all institute the Lord's Supper which we celebrate today, whether it be in Wittenberg, Rome, or Geneva. And at the same time we must add that none of these forms is fully without a tie to Jesus—even if this tie can only be demonstrated through a much-involved tradition-history.

Theological and Practical
Consequences

We come now to the question of the consequences—systematic-dogmatic, and also practical—of what has been presented.

On one point there should be unanimity at the very outset. Even if the development here portrayed would prove inaccurate or inexact, there could still be no doubt that the Lord's Supper did pass through a development which begins not just after the New Testament, but whose beginning can be traced already within—and even before—the New Testament.

It is not possible, however, to place the various stages of a development alongside each other in order to ask for *the* Lord's Supper in the New Testament (not in its succession of stages, but in its composite). There is no *one* Lord's Supper in the New Testament; there are various Lord's Suppers and there is a history of the Lord's Supper. The different Lord's Suppers cannot be harmonized, because the various stages of a development cannot be harmonized. What comes out is always a distorted picture.

Hence, it is not surprising that in the history of the church and of Christian doctrine, right up to the present day, there are so many, various understandings of the Lord's Supper. To be sure, there are many impulses which have played their part. The thought categories which are used in assertions differ for different times and places. But these thought categories tend to determine not only the concepts of the Lord's Supper of their own time, but also always have their influence on the church tradition that follows. The Roman Catholic Church cannot move behind the Aristotelian definitions of the Fourth Lateran Council of 1215; and discussion of the Arnoldshain theses[69] shows how strongly

69. [Statements on the meaning of the Lord's Supper worked out by Reformed and Lutheran theologians at Arnoldshain, Germany, in 1957; cf. E. M. Skibble, "Discussion of Intercommunion in German Protestantism," *The Lutheran Quarterly*, 11 (1959), 91-111, and "Reaction to the Arnoldshain Theses on the Lord's Supper," *ibid.*, 12 (1960), 249-55; and Egil Grislis, "The Arnoldshain Theses on the Lord's Supper in Recent Discussion," *ibid.*, 13 (1961),333-55. —EDITOR.]

in Protestantism the formulations of the Reformation period continue
not only to have an effect, but also to shape present statements.

To reach a consensus today is more difficult because one can no
longer simply appeal to the New Testament. For there is no such thing
as *the* New Testament witness about the Lord's Supper, nor can one just
ask about the "decisive" witness if one has not decided what is now to be
decisive and what not.

Thus we come to realize that the problem of the Lord's Supper in the
last analysis is not a problem of the Lord's Supper at all, but the problem of the proper use of Scripture. Thus we shall never come to a
consensus as long as we are not ready to come to grips with another
relationship to the New Testament, in fact that very one which lies in
the New Testament itself.

The New Testament is the history of a proclamation; it is the oldest
history (preserved) of Christian proclamation. But this proclamation
already reflects a theological (*dogmengeschichtliche*) development. It
is not as though the history of Christian doctrine begins only after the
New Testament; rather, it already runs through the New Testament
itself. And its beginning lies already before the New Testament. If that
is accepted (and there is no real reason why it should not be), we have
also found a way to get out of the becalmed area.

Let us clarify this by reflecting on the problem of preaching. A
sermon expounds a text, which lies "before" it. If one is really to get at
the heart of the matter (*die Sache*), he may not in the last resort be
directed by the *exposition* of the matter (that is to say, by the sermons
summarized in the New Testament) but must make an effort to get
back through the exposition to the matter itself. Of course, I always
have the matter only as expounded; but it is never formulated once for
all since the exposition is always a limited attempt—limited and conditioned by its age—to bring the matter to expression. A new attempt
must be made by men who live in another age.

If we are right in what we have been saying about the celebration of
the meal before its meaning had come to be explained, these aspects
appear to be significant; the Lord's Supper is the celebration by a community which, through Jesus, regards itself as an eschatological community. The members express their common bond as an eschatological
congregation at their celebration and by it; they experience it, it shapes
them. In the meal (as in the accounts about meals which we encounter
in the Synoptic tradition) they anticipate the eschatological meal. This

is thus nothing other than the reality of the new age, given through Jesus, amid the old age which is passing away.

In an era and an environment where people celebrated such reality in the mystery cults, where they were convinced they could hold on to such reality only when they thought of it as transmitted in the form of "matter" and therefore tied to "elements," this development sketched above could be a thoroughly appropriate expression for the intention of the original—in spite of all the problems that we today might find in it.

But we must realize that it is a matter here of *one* interpretation of the "meal in action"; and we cannot and may not take this interpretation as foundation for our understanding of the meal. We simply cannot escape making our own interpretation, though we must realize that it is not possible for us to go back directly to the original. That is not possible because every interpretation—ours included!—is not only conditioned by the text which it interprets, but is at the same time influenced by the history of interpretation through the centuries.

No one who tries today to interpret anew the Lord's Supper of Jesus (or more accurately, Jesus' table fellowship) can disregard the fact that he himself has already celebrated the Lord's Supper in the church and consequently brings along certain set notions. Whether he takes these over is indeed another question. He can also correct them. But even if he makes a correction, he is still influenced by his earlier conceptions. It would be erroneous to suppose that one could leap out of his own tradition in order to find a completely new point of beginning.

I would suggest that we have now fixed the two reference points with which practical theology has to do: namely, the systematic working out of the exegetical content, *and* the practice of the church (down to the present), which has been developed in and through the tradition.

Easy and final solutions cannot be quickly proposed here. They can grow out of further fundamental reflection. Thus the following considerations I shall make not in the form of assertions, but as questions, which admittedly are "slanted" questions and ones in which I hint at the direction in which the answers are to be sought.

(1) Is a celebration of the Lord's Supper possible in the fortuitous gathering of a Sunday morning congregation? People scarcely know each other. The only tie is that between the individual and the altar; the human relationship necessary for the Lord's Supper is missing, however. Can the character of the eschatological congregation (as "new covenant") find living expression in this way?

The way our celebrations of the Lord's Supper are conducted seems —at least to me—to contradict this. The mood surely is not that of eschatological joy, not the joy that comes from belonging *here* to the eschatological congregation. Thus this question arises: Is the Lord's Supper not really a celebration which (at least in our present ecclesiastical situation) belongs in "circles" such as family, congregation (*Gemeindekreise*), specific assemblies (*Konvente*), student groups, leisure-time groups, etc.?

(2) Is not the fellowship character of the meal lost by people coming to the altar individually or in groups? Are they not still receiving "holy food" at the altar? The altar is no longer the table around which people sit.

If it is no longer possible (and very often, to be sure, it is not) to sit around the table, could not the fellowship be better expressed by letting the congregation remain seated and having helpers distribute bread and wine in the pews? This practice, which of course already exists in some groups, might bring to expression a decisive feature of the communion in a striking way.

(3) Even though I admit uncertainty here, I should nonetheless like to ask whether for us the meal still has such communicative power as it no doubt had for Judaism. Perhaps it does, but is consuming bread and wine a "meal"? Does taking a bit of bread and a sip of wine have the character of a meal?

Certainly the Lord's Supper does not depend only on these two things, bread and wine, as such. That it came to do so arises from the fact that prayers over the bread and the cup of blessing accentuated these two parts within a complete meal.

One must ask the even more fundamental question: Just how is reality communicated to *us*? With the Jews it was done historically; with the Greeks, materially; and with us . . . ?

At this point one would hardly want to supersede the tradition (that the Lord's Supper comes to us as a *meal*), nor perhaps could one. But at the same time we ought to ask how the reality of the gift is preserved at a meal.

I do not have an answer here, but I could imagine that we might develop a form of meal in which the community could experience what the Lord's Supper originally said and wanted to communicate. If that would happen, we would likely experience in a way completely different from what is generally the case today what community means and especially what eschatological community is.

What has been said may strike some as strange. If so, I beg you to weigh one thing more. This impression of strangeness arises not only from these remarks; it would also immediately arise if a Lutheran suddenly had to celebrate the Lord's Supper in Reformed fashion, or if a Protestant suddenly had to celebrate the Lord's Supper as a eucharistic sacrifice. Each individual understanding of the Lord's Supper more or less excludes the other understandings.

It should be clear that in the long run this is not bearable for a church that thinks ecumenically. We should be concerned to tear down the walls between the confessions. However, that is possible only when we are willing not only to examine other positions critically, but also do not exclude our own position from critical examination. Whoever truly desires ecumenicity must be prepared under the circumstances also himself to rethink positions.

When that happens, criteria and norms need to be found by which both one's own and other positions can be measured and tested. This discussion has been intended to serve that purpose.

My remarks are in no way meant to supply *the* solution. I do believe that what has been said is of a certain significance because here the problem of the Lord's Supper has not been treated in isolation, as is so often the case; rather, it has been set and studied in a relation to a series of other problems no less acute, problems such as Christology and Scripture.

It may be that this sketch will be helpful as a basis for discussion.

For Further

Reading

FOR FURTHER READING

BY WILLI MARXSEN

Introduction to the New Testament: An Approach to Its Problems. Translated by G. Buswell. Philadelphia: Fortress, 1968.

Mark the Evangelist: Studies on the Redaction History of the Gospel. Translated by Roy A. Harrisville et al. Nashville: Abingdon, 1969. There is a lengthy summary and critique in Joachim Rohde's book *Rediscovering the Teaching of the Evangelists.* Translated by Dorothea M. Barton. New Testament Library. London: SCM, 1968; Philadelphia; Westminster, 1969. Pp. 113-40.

"The Resurrection of Jesus as a Historical and Theological Problem." In *The Significance of the Message of the Resurrection for Faith in Jesus Christ,* edited and with an introduction by C. F. D. Moule, and translated by Dorothea M. Barton, pp. 15-50. Studies in Bible Theology, series 2, vol. 8. London: SCM, 1968. Pp. 15-50.

The Resurrection of Jesus of Nazareth. Translated by Margaret Kohl. Philadelphia: Fortress, 1970. In addition to reviews, see G. Friedrich. "Die Auferweckung Jesu, eine Tat Gottes oder ein Interpretament der Jünger?" *Kerygma und Dogma* 17 (1971): 153-87; and K. L. McKay. "Some Linguistic Points in Marxsen's Resurrection Theory." *Expository Times* 84 (1972-73): 330-32.

Marxsen's famous phrase, about how "the 'cause of Jesus' goes on," is discussed by F. J. Schierse ("Die 'Sache Jesu' — ein biblischer Begriff?" *Bibel und Leben* 4 [Düsseldorf, 1969]: 300-306), who affirms it and compares 1 Cor. 7:32 and Phil. 2:21; F. Mussner. "Die 'Sache Jesu.' " *Catholica* 25 (Münster, 1971): 81-89; Josef Nolte. "Die Sache Jesu und die Zukunft der Kirche." In *Jesus von Nazareth,* edited by F. J. Schierse, pp. 214-33. Mainz: Matthias-Grünewald-Verlag, 1972; W. Kasper. "Die Sache Jesu: Recht und Grenzen eines Interpretationsversuches." *Herder Korrespondenz* 26 (1972): 185-89; and N. M. Watson. " 'The Cause of Jesus Continues'? An Investigation of the Intention of Willi Marxsen." *Australian Biblical Review* 25 (1977): 21-28.

Der Exeget als Theologie: Vorträge zum Neuen Testament. Gütersloh: Gerd Mohn, 1968.

The New Testament as the Church's Book. Translated by James E. Mignard. Philadelphia: Fortress, 1972. Cf. A. J. M. Wedderburn. "The New Testament as the Church's Book?" *Scottish Journal of Theology* 31 (1978): 23-40.

"The Lord's Supper: Concepts and Developments." In *Jesus in His Time,* edited by Hans Jürgen Schultz, translated by Brian Watchorn, pp. 106-14. Philadelphia: Fortress, 1971.

"The New Testament: A Collection of Sermons. A Contribution to the Discussion on the Canon and to the Question of the Historical Jesus." *Modern Churchman* 19 (1976): 134-43.

"Die urchristlichen Kerygmata und das Ereignis Jesus von Nazareth." *Zeitschrift für Theologie und Kirche* 73 (1976): 42-64.

Die Sache Jesu geht weiter. Gütersloher Taschenbücher 112. Gütersloh: Gerd Mohn, 1976.

Christologie—praktisch. Gütersloher Taschenbücher 294. Gütersloh: Gerd Mohn, 1978.

ON THE SUBJECT OF THIS BOOK

In addition to titles mentioned in the footnotes, see:

ON THE SON OF MAN:

For survey of current views, see I. H. Marshall. "The Synoptic Son of Man Sayings in Recent Discussion." *New Testament Studies* 12 (1965-66): 327-51; Norman Perrin. *A Modern Pilgrimage in New Testament Christology.* Philadelphia: Fortress, 1974. Pp. 133-41; and *The Interpreter's Dictionary of the Bible.* Supplementary volume. S.v. "Son of Man."

Higgins, A. J. B. *Jesus and the Son of Man.* Philadelphia: Fortress, 1965.

Fuller, Reginald H. *The Foundations of New Testament Christology.* New York: Scribner's, 1965. Pp. 34-43, 65, 119-25, 151-55, 233-34.

Tödt, Heinz Eduard. *The Son of Man in the Synoptic Tradition.* Translated by Dorothea M. Barton. Philadelphia: Westminster, 1965. Bultmannian School: Jesus spoke of the Son of man only with reference to someone else, a figure who would come in the future.

Hahn, Ferdinand. *The Titles of Jesus in Christology: Their History in Early Christianity.* Translated by Harold Knight and George Ogg. London: Lutterworth, 1969; New York and Cleveland: World, 1969. Pp. 15-67.

ON FAITH:

See especially the literature noted above in essay 1, footnotes 50, 59, and 67.

Fuchs, Ernst. "Jesus and Faith." In *Studies of the Historical Jesus,* translated by Andrew Scobie, pp. 48-64. Studies in Biblical Theology, vol. 42. London: SCM, 1964.

The Interpreter's Dictionary of the Bible. Supplementary volume. S.v. "Faith, Faithlessness in the NT."

ON THE LORD'S SUPPER:

Lietzmann, Hans. *Mass and Lord's Supper: A Study in the History of the Liturgy.* With an introduction and supplementary essay by R. D. Richardson, and translated by Dorothea H. G. Reeve. Leiden: Brill, 1953-.

Jeremias, Joachim. *The Eucharistic Words of Jesus.* Translated from the 3d German ed. (1960) by Norman Perrin. New York: Scribner's 1966; Philadelphia: Fortress, 1977.

Schweizer, Eduard. *The Lord's Supper According to the New Testament.* Translated by James M. Davis. Facet Books Biblical Series, vol. 18. Philadelphia: Fortress, 1967. Bibliography, pp. 39–45.

Lohmeyer, Ernst. "Das Abendmahl in der Urgemeinde." *Journal of Biblical Literature* 56 (1937): 217–52.

Cullmann, Oscar, and Leenhardt, F. J. *Essays on the Lord's Supper.* Translated by J. G. Davies. Ecumenical Studies in Worship, vol. 1. London: Lutterworth, 1958; Richmond: John Knox, 1958.

Delling, Gerhard. "Abendmahl II: Urchristliches Mahl-Verständnis." In *Theologische Realenzyklopädie,* vol. 1, edited by G. Krause et al., pp. 47–58. Berlin and New York: Walter de Gruyter, 1977.